NATURE
ON THE
RAMPAGE

WITH

H. J. DE BLIJ

NATURE
ON THE
RAMPAGE

WITH
H. J. DE BLIJ

SMITHSONIAN
BOOKS
WASHINGTON, D.C.

NATURE ON THE RAMPAGE

Produced by

THE ROLAND COMPANY

Producer and Editor   David Roland

Art Director and Picture Editor   Charles O. Hyman

Book and Graphic Designer   Kevin Osborn

Copy Editors   Blair Burns Potter, Janice D.H. Roland

Indexer   Robert Elwood

THE SMITHSONIAN INSTITUTION

Secretary   I. Michael Heyman

Secretary Emeritus   Robert McC. Adams

Assistant Secretary for External Affairs   Thomas E. Lovejoy

Director, Smithsonian Institution Press   Felix C. Lowe

SMITHSONIAN BOOKS

Editor-in-Chief   Patricia Gallagher

Senior Editor   Alexis Doster III

Editors   Amy Donovan, Joe Goodwin

Associate Editors   Bryan D. Kennedy, Sonia Reece

Assistant Editor   Robert Lockhart

Editorial Intern   Theresa Gradishar

Senior Picture Editor   Frances C. Rowsell

Picture Editors   Carrie E. Bruns, R. Jenny Takacs

Picture Research   Laura Kreiss

Production Editor   Patricia Upchurch

Business Manager   Stephen J. Bergstrom

Marketing Manager   Susan E. Romatowski

Distributed to the trade by Login Publishers Consortium.

ISBN 0-89599-048-2 (Smithsonian Books)

Library of Congress Cataloging-in-Publication Data

Nature on the rampage / with Harm De Blij.
        p.   cm.
    Includes index.
        ISBN 0-89599-048-2. — ISBN 0-89599-049-0 (pbk.)
        1. Natural disasters.   I. De Blij, Harm J.
    GB5014.N39   1994
    363.3'4—dc20
                                                    94-23115
                                                        CIP

CONTENTS

NATURE ON THE RAMPAGE

H. J. DE BLIJ

THE NATURAL ENVIRONMENT is both humanity's ally and its adversary. Its bounty sustains billions. Its rampages have killed millions. Many of us continue to live near active volcanoes, in perilous flood plains, on earthquake-prone slopes. We inhabit such danger zones despite the risks, because traditional livelihoods impel it. Our hominid ancestors suffered nature's caprices with little protection and less preparation, so human evolution is the story of adaptation or extinction. The lineage that led to *Homo sapiens* survived several million years of environmental fluctuation in its African domicile as conditions swung from warm, moist, and forested to cold, dry, and treeless back to warmth again. Scientists used to believe that such climatic alternations came gradually, allowing for slow adjustment for survival. Now we know that nature moves fast, posing a continuous threat that often translates into sudden disaster.

Our instinct for territoriality is matched by a wariness of nature's power, gained over countless generations of coping with change. Today that wariness recedes as we have technologies that enable us to live in frigid latitudes and in barren deserts, on polar ice and on artificial islands. And yet nature on the rampage continues to take its human toll, and to threaten our very existence.

THE PACE OF CHANGE

Early in the twentieth century, a debate raged among scientists over the processes that transform the face of the Earth. The scientific community was divided between those who argued that slow, continuous, and inexorable change produced the landscapes we admire today and those who interpreted the evidence differently. The "gradualists" theorized that the effect of any rare and sudden natural event would soon be erased by a return to equilibrium. The "catastrophists" argued that hurricanes, earthquakes, volcanic eruptions, and other dramatic events did far more to permanently change the surface than any long-term processes could.

The gradualists won the day, and theirs became the preferred view. Not until recent years has the notion of catastrophism again come to the fore. In part this revival has been due to discoveries concerning extinctions—not only the now-famous K/T boundary, marking a cataclysmic event that took place between the Cretaceous and Tertiary periods some 67 million years ago and led to the demise of many dinosaur species, but also earlier and later incidents that changed the planet instantly and permanently. Evidence from ice cores, ocean floors, volcanic strata, delta beds, and other sources has confirmed nature's capacity to go on the rampage and change the world.

As is so often the case when a philosophical debate of this kind occurs, both sides have merit. The gradualists were correct on one major point: nature's ability to repair damage to its environmental systems and its eventual return to equilibrium following catastrophic events. During massive volcanic eruptions associated with the collision of tectonic plates, huge quantities of gases, dust, and other pollutants were spewed into the atmosphere in brief bursts of activity. Global weather was modified and overall environments everywhere changed quickly.

Yet the atmosphere in time cleansed itself, the sun broke through again, photosynthesis resumed, plants and animals recovered, and normal atmospheric functions were restored. We witnessed a minor version of such events when Mount Pinatubo in the Philippines erupted in 1991. Scientists concluded that this single volcano's activity was responsible for an interruption of enhanced greenhouse-warming trends. But when the supercontinent of Pangaea broke apart 200 million years ago and the continental landmasses we know today started drifting outward from Africa, the accompanying volcanic activity dwarfed anything familiar to us. The lava that poured from the fissures created plateaus that still exist: India's Deccan is one; Africa's Victoria Falls plunge off another. Yet life on Earth did not end. The atmosphere survived and recovered.

With respect to equilibrium, the gradualists noted nearly a century ago how a storm-damaged coast could be restored by years of renewed action by waves and currents. From this and other observations they concluded that a more general environmental equilibrium would be achieved in all situations, for example, after periods of glaciation. And, indeed, Earth has witnessed some 6,000 years of comparative environmental stability during the current warm, interglacial period we know as the Holocene epoch. But nature may be hinting at change to come.

Over the past millennium, as the following pages record, the environmental pendulum has been swinging more widely again. Scientists refer to the cooling and warming cycles of the past thousand years as the Little Ice Age, and the recent greenhouse-warming episode may be just the most recent phase of it. There is evidence that the reversal of cycles has been accompanied by severe climatic swings and powerful weather extremes. The recent record suggests that such a time has come again.

MAINTAINING PERSPECTIVE

The environmental register also compels us to view the world in spatial—that is, geographic—context. We continue to extrapolate regional events into global conditions, but in fact our planet habitually sends out contradictory signals as if to purposely confuse us. The greenhouse warming alert of the 1980s was based substantially on weather extremes recorded in North America (notably eastern North America) and parts of Western Europe; records in other areas of the world, notably in the Southern Hemisphere, were inconsistent with the northern experience. The climatic swings and weather extremes described in the pages that follow should, therefore, be seen in a regional perspective.

As recently as June 1994, record-shattering heat afflicted southern Pakistan and northwestern India while temperatures in the U.S. Southwest set records exceeding 120 degrees Fahrenheit in a wide area from western Texas to southern California. Even as these regions simmered, Western Europe was experiencing one of its coldest springs on record, and cruise ships were being turned away from routine springtime itineraries to Newfoundland because of icebergs—the latest known dates for this danger at such low latitudes.

A spatial interpretation of the available record suggests that global warming and cooling are misnomers, and that global environmental swings are inconsistent, even contradictory, in regional context. This means that reconstructions of past ice-age environments in low-latitude settings will be exceptionally difficult. For example, a non-geographic perspective might suggest that polar glaciations had the effect of cooling (and drying) the tropical regions where hominids evolved. But correlating known glacial pulses with sudden swings of East African environments may not be so simple. When the ice sheets repeatedly spread over present-day Canada and the Midwest, East Africa may not have mirrored these cycles, at least not consistently. It may not always have become cool in Africa when it got cold in North America, a consideration which must be taken into account as we attempt to understand human evolution. Despite global trends, regions tend to exhibit discrete environmental character. And, as so often is the case, spatial variation—geography—is a key to comprehension.

DANGER FROM ABOVE

Earth is about 4.7 billion years old, which makes it, as heavenly bodies go, relatively young. Congealed from an orbiting mass of cosmic matter, it had not even developed a solid crust when, a mere 100 million years into its existence, it had an encounter that would shape its future forevermore. A large asteroid crossed its path, dealt it a glancing blow that tore off a section of its surface, and, burdened by this extra weight, failed to escape its gravitational field. The Moon, orbiting just a few hundred miles from the molten, wave-roiled earthly surface, filled the sky. Its impact had set our planet spinning so wildly that a "day" lasted just four hours. As time went on, the Moon receded to a more distant orbit (its orbital distance from Earth continues to increase very slightly every year). Earth's rotation slowed down, and a solid crust, 70 percent of it submerged under a global ocean, developed.

How Earth survived this cataclysmic event and what its lasting consequences were remain unanswered questions. Is the encounter related to the inclination of Earth's axis of rotation to the plane of its solar orbit? Is it the source of the "wobble" of the rotational axis that may, in turn, affect environmental variations to this day? Did it set up currents of motion in the molten Earth that had the capacity to move slabs of the solid crust once these formed? To these, and to many other questions relating to the lunar impact, there are no final answers yet.

Since Earth acquired the Moon, numerous

asteroids have struck the planet; one such impact may have caused the demise of the dinosaurs (a suspect crater lies buried under sediments in Yucatán). Earth's surface is pocked with evidence of other collisions; some, like Meteor Crater in Arizona, are starkly visible in the landscape today. In 1908, Europe's major cities barely escaped disaster when the Tunguska meteoroid struck the eastern side of Russia's Ural Mountains, an event long hidden from view by the then-ongoing revolution and by subsequent Soviet concealment.

The Moon's crater-sculpted surface reminds us of the protective cushion Earth's atmosphere provides—but some asteroids and meteoroids do penetrate it and strike the surface. In recent years, astronomers have expressed growing concern about the threat posed by the large number of asteroids that inhabit the space through which Earth hurtles along its orbit around the Sun. Some have proposed a program of research aimed at developing the ability to divert or pulverize such objects.

This, perhaps, is nature's most intimidating threat: a bombardment from space that could lay waste to cities, even regions, without warning. The available evidence indicates that even a comparatively small specimen can create major damage. Arizona's Meteor Crater was made by an object estimated to have been no larger than a trailer truck. Yet its diameter averages 4,000 feet and its upwarped rim lies more than 750 feet above the crater floor—a space big enough to hold the downtown area of a sizable city. On the positive side, about 70 percent of Earth's surface is water, so a meteoroid that does penetrate all the way through the atmosphere has only a 30 percent chance of hitting land (much of which is desert or forest or otherwise sparsely peopled). Nevertheless, nature's threat from space has great destructive potential, and no adequate means of prediction or preparation exist.

DANGER FROM BELOW

While the catastrophists and the gradualists were debating, a geographer named Alfred Wegener was busy starting another scientific argument. In 1912 he published a book optimistically entitled *The Origin of Continents and Oceans* in which he hypothesized that an ancient supercontinent had existed until about 200 million years ago. About that time, Wegener theorized, continental drift tore this landmass apart. (Wegener called the land Pangaea; the northern half was Laurasia and the southern half Gondwanaland.) The present continents are the resulting pieces, still drifting outward from the heart of Pangaea, which was Africa.

Wegener's notion was rejected by many geologists, especially in the United States, until after midcentury. But for others he set a research agenda that was to lead to the identification of the crustal slabs (plates) that form Earth's lithosphere, and to the discovery of plate tectonics, the process that moves them. The continents do indeed drift, but not in the way Wegener envisaged. They are carried piggyback on moving plates.

The movement of crustal plates, driven by subcrustal, circulating cells of molten and viscous rock kept boiling by heat from continuing chemical reactions, creates zones of instability and danger around the world. In certain zones, plates are pulled away from each other and lava fills the fissures, creating new crust. In other zones, they collide, crushing, bending, folding, and breaking rock strata in the process. We do not see much of the former, because the great fissures where new crust is formed traverse the ocean floors (which is why tectonic plate movement is often called seafloor spreading).

Deep beneath the ocean surface, along the Mid-Atlantic Ridge and along thousands of miles of submarine fissures elsewhere, a great drama plays itself out as deep-seated, red-hot magma oozes into the space between separating plates, boiling the ocean water as it solidifies as lava. In the warmth of the water nearby lives a submarine fauna only recently seen, sustained by these unique conditions. Some scientists suggest that this may be the place to look for clues to the origin of life on Earth.

Only in Africa today can crustal spreading (a better name for the process) be seen as it probably was when Pangaea broke apart. Africa's steep-sided rift valleys, some filled with water, may represent the final phase of the supercontinent's fragmentation. The Red Sea has filled the rift that split the Arabian Peninsula from Africa; East Africa, like Arabia, probably will form a discrete plate as well, carrying that region, Madagascar-like, eastward. The heart of Pangaea seems finally poised to fracture.

Dramatic as this sequence may be, plate separation is much less destructive to people and property than plate collision. Where plates converge, the ground is literally swallowed up. Heavier rock sinks downward into and below the crust, where it is remolten and recycled. Lighter rock is pushed upward, forming mountain chains such as South America's Andes and the spectacular scenery along Alaska's coast. All this is accompanied by earthquakes, so a world map of earthquake epicenters is also a map of plate-collision zones. And where the crust is rendered unstable this way, lava penetrates to the surface, often building great cratered peaks that loom, snow-covered, over the countryside. A map of active and dormant volcanoes looks very much like one of earthquakes, which is why Earth's most active crustal zone, encircling the world's largest ocean, is call the Pacific Ring of Fire.

It might as well be called the Ring of Fear. Hundreds of millions of people live at risk on the Pacific Ring, from Chile to Alaska and from Japan to New Zealand. The pages that follow show how such risk often translates into disaster.

Amazingly, California, is one of the safer segments on the Pacific Ring. There, two plates—the Pacific and the North American—neither collide nor separate, but slide past each other; the infamous San Andreas Fault marks that relatively benign contact. Such lateral motion can cause earthquakes, but the absence of volcanism from the California scene lessens the hazard.

Another zone of frequent earthquakes and intermittent volcanism stretches from Portugal to Papua New Guinea across southern Eurasia and into the Pacific. The great Himalaya Mountains are a unique part of it: here, two plates composed of similar rock create a giant dome. Because neither the Eurasian nor the Indo-Australian plate is made of the heavy rock that would sink downward, the two giant plates are both on an upward course, neither yielding to the other. The world's most spectacular mountain scenery results.

If the map of earthquake incidence is a reliable indicator of earthquake threat, and if the threat is confined to plate-contact zones, then people who want to be safe from earthquakes ought to be able to find a haven by looking at the map. Unfortunately, nature often has the unexpected up her sleeve: in this instance, something geologists call intraplate earthquakes, quakes that strike not the colliding edges, but the supposedly stable interiors of crustal plates. The two strongest earthquakes ever recorded in the contiguous United States, for example, were centered in Missouri and South Carolina, not California. In 1976, an intraplate earthquake near the Chinese city of Tangshan claimed what some estimate to have been as many as 750,000 lives. Since then, Australia and India have experienced this frightening phenomenon as well, and clearly no place on Earth is totally safe from it.

Volcanic eruptions have changed the course of human history. One of them, the explosive eruption of Mount Toba on the Indonesian island of Sumbawa, may have come close to extinguishing humanity altogether. This blast, about 74,000 years ago, created what archaeologists call an evolutionary bottleneck—a severe worsening of environmental conditions already affected by the bitter cold of the most recent glaciation—that resulted in the eradication of great numbers of our ancestors. Nothing like this had happened for perhaps a million years or more; nothing like it has happened since, although the explosion of Thíra (Santorini) at the height of Minoan culture certainly helped shape history.

Volcanoes often give warning of their intent, but they may also erupt unexpectedly. Santorini apparently gave warning, unlike Vesuvius in A.D. 79; no skeletons evincing sudden death have been found on the island. But whether a volcano threatens or not, people will persist in living on its flanks, just as they do in earthquake-prone areas. The great city of Tokyo lies in one of the world's most vulnerable environmental locales—where three tectonic plates collide, an active volcano stands offshore, and Fuji rises nearby. About every 70 years since the 1630s, Tokyo has been struck, but the city never stops growing. The Pacific Rim is a place of opportunity as well as catastrophe; the latter is soon forgotten, while the former pervades it.

Recently, scientists have come to realize that the breakup of Pangaea was only the latest fragmentation of a supercontinent in Earth's history. Now it is known that the divergence and convergence of landmasses go on continuously. Pangaea may have had as many as four predecessors, each broken up and subsequently reassembled. By some calculations, the outward motion of the present plate-carried continents has already slowed down so much that it will soon (geologically speaking) stop. Eventually, the landmasses will start converging on Africa again. In North America, the West Coast will flatten out, and California-like scenery will develop in the East as the Atlantic Ocean narrows and the continent moves toward Africa.

How long does a complete cycle of divergence and reassembly take? It has taken approximately 200 million years for Pangaea's landmasses to reach their present position; they may continue to move outward for another 20 million years. After a period of standstill, they may take about as long to reassemble. A complete cycle, therefore, may take over 500 million years. The process of plate tectonics thus may have begun soon after the first slabs of solid rock, the continental shields, formed from the molten surface more than 3 billion years ago.

AN ICY FUTURE?

Before Pangaea broke apart, the supercontinent was cooled by an ice age that left its evidence in Africa, South America, India, and Australia. That evidence was among Alfred Wegener's most convincing substantiation that a unified Pangaea had indeed existed. Now evidence is accumulating that previous supercontinents, too, were glaciated before they split up. Today, with the landmasses nearly as far as they are likely to diverge, the Earth is again experiencing an ice age. Might this mean that ice ages develop in some sort of synchrony with the plate-tectonic cycle?

There is not enough evidence to be sure. What is beyond doubt, though, is that Pangaea glaciated for tens of millions of years prior to its breakup, and now another ice age prevails. For more than 20 million years, the current ice age has periodically cooled the planet, first forming the great Antarctic ice sheet and then, as its cold phases deepened, creating great continental glaciers in the Northern Hemisphere. At least twice, average temperatures dropped precipitously. The most recent decline took place between 3.0 and 2.5 million years ago, marking the onset of the Pleistocene phase of this ice age. The

Pleistocene has witnessed more than two dozen rapid advances of the ice, followed by brief, often intense warm spells. Overall, cold has reigned supreme: a frigid glaciation tends to last 100,000 years on average, a warm phase about 11,000.

The entire story of modern civilization— the domestication of plants and animals, the building of cities, the formation of states— has occurred during the current warm phase. The retreat of the glaciers opened much of the Earth for human habitation: barely more than 13,000 years ago, ice covered the heart of North America, and much of Europe was tundra. Even so, we live today under unusually salubrious conditions. The Holocene has held its surprises, including a sudden surge of cold when loads of melting glacial ice poured into the North Atlantic. But from about 7,000 to 1,000 years ago, things were relatively calm. Not until about 1,000 years ago did things begin to stir again.

Toward the end of the tenth century, Earth appears to have been as warm as it is today, possibly even warmer. In the Northern Hemisphere, permanent settlements, including farms, were established on Iceland and Greenland, and along these stepping stones Leif Eriksson and his party reached North America. Simultaneously, the South Pacific Ocean grew calm enough to allow the Maori to reach New Zealand's shores. Vineyards thrived in Britain and the Rhine region. Sea levels were high and rising, and the Dutch learned to build dikes to protect polders.

There are parallels between this warm, calm end of the tenth century and the end of the twentieth. Probably no one a thousand years ago had any idea that good times would come to an end. When they did, it was so sudden that much human dislocation resulted. The Viking settlements on Greenland were extinguished as winters grew frigid and summers stayed cold. The British wine industry was destroyed in a

matter of years. The limit of agriculture was driven southward as much as 200 miles. Storms roiled seas that had been avenues of contact. Weather extremes abounded. The environment was reversing course: it was the beginning of the Little Ice Age, and nature was on the rampage.

Available records tell us that the Little Ice Age has been marked by wide swings of climate punctuated by periods of what can only be described as environmental chaos. Since the middle of the nineteenth century, an overall, though not consistent, warming trend has prevailed. When this warming trend was interrupted during the 1950s and 1960s, scientists warned that a return to colder times might lie ahead, but few extremes marked this transition and the warning was soon forgotten. Climatic records indicate a resumption of warming from the late 1970s until the early 1990s, and warnings that human enhancement of greenhouse warming might set off a global environmental crisis gained credibility.

Nature, however, may have something else in store for our planet. The recent cooling-warming alternation may presage conditions similar to those prevailing a thousand years ago; the warm spell now in progress has lasted about as long as the two others preceding it. In just the past several years, we have seen the number of weather extremes grow: an unprecedented drought in Africa, the flood of the millennium in the Midwest and the blizzard of the century in the East and Southeast, both in 1993, and a 1994 winter so bitter that visions of a new ice age swept the warnings of greenhouse warming off the front pages. If these are indeed nature's early warning of an environment reversal, the following pages illustrate what lies ahead. In the context of the Holocene, our works have been tested only slightly by nature's whim. In the perspective of a full-scale return to glaciation, we have not been tested at all.

WEATHER'S FURY

RICHARD LIPKIN

A HUMID BREEZE wafted along Key Biscayne beach on the evening of Friday, August 21, 1992. Teenagers hurled frisbees, foamy waves lapped the shore, and dusk set a peach-striped sky aglow.

It seemed to be just another weekend getting under way in Dade County, Florida. Except for the sea gulls. The white birds appeared to vanish, as they often do when a great storm nears land.

Far over the Atlantic horizon, more than 1,000 miles southeast, an Air Force weather reconnaissance plane stood refueling on the tarmac in Antigua, an elegant island in the Caribbean's Lesser Antilles. Lieutenant Colonel Gale Carter, chief meteorologist of the 53rd Weather Reconnaissance Squadron, climbed aboard the instrument-packed Lockheed WC-130 and gave the nod to go. The pilot taxied the plane onto the runway, spun its four propellers for takeoff, and lifted the modified cargo craft into the evening sky.

Carter and his crew of six "Hurricane Hunters" soared to 23,000 feet and headed for airspace northeast of Puerto Rico, where Tropical Storm Andrew was brewing. With churning clouds in sight, the pilot descended to 10,000 feet, then penetrated the storm. This routine 11-hour mission to "check out the storm," as Carter said, called for a crisscross flight

through the gale's turbulent center to measure its wind speed, pressure, temperature, and humidity.

Just after midnight, in the eye of the storm, the crew ejected a sonde—a tube of weather instruments suspended by a parachute—from the plane's underbelly. Falling 1,000 feet a minute, the sonde radioed back a low pressure of 994 millibars. On the storm's far side, the crew measured a wind speed above 94 miles per hour. Time for a storm status upgrade, Carter decided.

On the radio to forecasters at the National Hurricane Center in Coral Gables, Florida, Carter reported, "We've got a hurricane here— but it's barely a hurricane. I'm not even sure it's gonna last."

Meanwhile, the meteorologists were picking up strange, mixed signals from Andrew. No one really knew what it would do. With a weakly organized core, the hurricane just might dissipate in the North Atlantic, or it could swell into a demonic gale. Over the next 24 hours, scientists scrambled to predict Andrew's trajectory. Hurricane advisories ticked on the news wire. Telephone calls went out to emergency managers. Radio and television announcers broadcasted storm warnings.

On Sunday night, hundreds of thousands of Floridians followed the storm advisories and fled north. In darkness all along South Dixie Highway, slicker-clad policemen directed traffic in stinging rain. Whether to a relative's upstate home, an Alabama motel, or a church atrium, Dade County homeowners barreled north on Interstate 95 for hundreds of miles.

It was after midnight when hell came to visit Dade County. By 3 A.M. Monday, winds above 100 miles per hour began to punch through windows, snap trees, flip trucks, and rip roofs off homes. Boats and planes were dragged across fields and piled up on lawns. In Andrew's grip, mobile homes crumpled like tin cans. In flood-

Above, a view inside Typhoon Sarah, taken from a Lockheed P-3 Orion weather plane in 1986, reveals the calm, circular center of the storm.

Right, computer-generated, multi-spectral image of Hurricane Andrew shows the trajectory of the storm system as it leaves behind a ravaged southern Florida and heads towards Louisiana.

Opposite, a photo of Hurricane Elena's dense swirling cloud mass taken by a crew member aboard space shuttle *Discovery* during a September 1985 mission.

Page 20: A mountain of twisted metal and stacked yachts is all that remains of this Charleston, South Carolina, marina demolished by Hurricane Hugo on September 21, 1989.

Pages 22-23: Florida motorists run a gauntlet of flying debris and falling trees as they try to navigate a main thoroughfare during the height of Hurricane Andrew's 145- to 175-mile-an-hour winds on August 24, 1992.

Pages 24-25: A twin-engine airplane hurled into trees on the perimeter of an airfield in Kingston, Jamaica, by Hurricane Gilbert on September 12, 1988.

Right, the concentric rings of ice visible in this cross section of a Michigan hailstone reveal its layered formation.

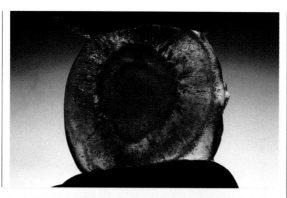

Above, the air above the equator, heated and set in motion by solar radiation and twisted by Earth's rotation, produces the constant weather changes that develop in the mid-latitudes. The spiral cloud systems are cyclones, which rotate around an area of low pressure, and the bands of clouds are fronts marking the boundary between two air masses.

Right, Charles Greeley Abbot, fifth Secretary of the Smithsonian Institution in Washington, D.C., explains in this 1970 photo a section of his 18-foot chart recording 104 years of precipitation in St. Louis.

prone Miami suburbs, such as Homestead and Florida City, some residents decided to ride out the storm. Huddled in bathrooms or cellars, without electricity and heat, twitching at the sounds of roofs splintering, doors crunching, glass shattering, many storm-weary souls later said they shivered for hours with a fear they had never imagined.

High overhead in the reconnaissance plane, Carter and his crew pitched and tossed as gusts exceeding 195 miles per hour buffeted the plane. While Andrew intensified and headed toward Florida, the hurricane crews had continued flying their grueling missions. Back and forth they crisscrossed through Andrew's angry eye. "The roughest ride I'd ever had," said Carter. "Terrible turbulence rode us up, then dropped us down hundreds of feet in a few seconds." At one point, caught in a whipping downdraft, Carter had to push his head off the cockpit ceiling. Ocean-rich updrafts spawned severe thunderstorms whose intense lightning lit up the eye's gray interior. Soft, pea-sized hail pelted the plane's windshield, its electrical charge bringing the bluish glow of St. Elmo's fire to dance on the window pane. Rain struck with the force of a firehose, muffling the engine's sound, and solid sheets of water blurred the pilot's view.

At 5:05 A.M. Monday, the storm rumbled over land. Briefly it weakened, then came back full force, pumped by powerful winds focused into what some scientists now describe as tornado-like funnels, fueled by falling air pressure. Over Dade County, Andrew's ferocity actually increased. The storm's lowest recorded pressure, a startling 27.23 inches of mercury (normal atmospheric pressure is 29.92), was measured not by federal meteorologists but by an amateur observer named Mrs. Hall, who had hunkered down in the home her grandfather built from coral rock and concrete in 1945.

From the weather plane, Carter peered down

and saw whole neighborhoods blacken at once. Strange blue flashes darted across the townscape, as the wind whipped live power lines about "like flashcubes popping in the dark," Carter recalled. In a grand finale, blackness followed a great blue flash, as lightning felled a power-grid transformer.

An hour before Monday's dawn, even the forecasters felt fear. A 164-mile-per-hour wind shook the 12-story Hurricane Center. The ventilation system seized. Electricity stopped. Ceiling lights went out. An emergency generator resuscitated the computers. Then the sound of ripping metal filled the control room. A rotating radar antenna, housed beneath a protective dome, was torn from its rooftop mount.

Andrew's fiercest wind blasted only four hours in Florida before moving on to the Gulf of Mexico and finally Louisiana. By sunrise Monday in Dade County, the worst had passed. By noon, drizzle fell from gray skies.

It took much longer, though, for Dade County to settle down. Cautiously, survivors emerged from shelters and wandered through rubble, guided by police with maps since familiar trees, storefronts, and signposts no longer existed. An anxious silence soon set in. Mosquitoes buzzed. Humidity hovered over soaked remains, while the scorching tropical Sun steamed mattresses, toasters, and underwear hanging on smashed boards. The stench of mildew and rotting food filled the air. A homeless police officer muttered that "it looked like an atomic bomb" had struck.

For months, residents sifted through belongings while insurance companies settled claims. The grim human totals: 15 people dead as a direct result of the storm in Florida, eight in Louisiana, three in the Bahamas. Indirectly, Andrew took 39 more lives. The storm also destroyed roughly 25,000 homes, damaged 100,000 more, and left 250,000 people temporarily homeless. Total property damage exceeded $25 billion. Whole Florida neighbor-

hoods were wiped out. Ironically, more people were injured repairing their homes than fleeing or fighting the storm. In Andrew's immediate wake, no official help arrived. Emergency manager Kate Hale had to rail on national television to rally the aid brigade: "Where the hell is the cavalry on this one? We need food. We need water. We need people. For God's sake, where are they?"

WHAT IS WEATHER?

It has been said that life exists not only above Earth's oceans, but also below its atmospheric sea, which extends more than 50 miles above the oceans before dwindling into outer space. Stratified into three main layers—a low-lying troposphere, midrange stratosphere, and high-flying mesosphere—the air is always moving, its layers spawning great swirls, eddies, whirlpools, and turbulent streams.

The first 10 miles of atmosphere above sea level is where weather mostly occurs. Earth's nearest star showers its blue-green planet with light and heat, baking and bubbling the air into patterns. Despite billions of untraceable factors, weather largely boils down to a few simple principles. Warm, moist air tends to rise, while cold dry air tends to sink. Water tends to evaporate. And air tends to spiral into low pressure—and out of high pressure—zones. Thus the Sun's energy sets wind and waves in motion. Because the spinning planet tilts to one side, whole oceans and continents are warmed as others chill down, causing huge air masses to warm, expand, and rise, while others cool, contract, and sink.

Ocean waters evaporate and rise high into the cold winds, where tiny ice particles coalesce into clouds. Eventually storms form, raining excess water back to land and sea, yielding lightning from charged particles along the way. Through this process, thunderstorms, tornadoes, and hurricanes are born, as warm, moist breezes collide with cold, dry wind. Together they can whip

A weather observer with the Langmuir Laboratory for Atmospheric Research releases an instrument package into thunderclouds over South Baldy peak near the town of Socorro, New Mexico. The instruments measure the electric field beneath and within a cloud, and relay that data, via telemetry, to the nearby lab.

Workers, right, attach plywood to a South Florida storefront in preparation for the August 24, 1992, arrival of Hurricane Andrew.

Above, empty supermarket shelves await restocking after being laid bare by customers who heeded the advanced warnings about Allen, a hurricane that pounded the Texas coast in 1980.

A sign on south Padre Island, Texas, right, announces the customary hurricane party usually held by venturesome individuals who choose to ride out the storm—in this case, Hurricane Allen.

Opposite, maintenance worker Dave Foley faces one of the monster waves that crashed through the patio doors of a Jupiter Island, Florida, beachfront home on October 31, 1991. The waves were produced when energy from a 600-mile-wide storm off New England's coast combined with winds from Hurricane Grace.

around each other, occasionally spiraling into grand hurricanes or fast spinning tornadoes, much as water swirls down a drain.

This process of energy accumulation and release, yielding inclement weather, goes on constantly. At any moment, some 2,000 storms are under way globally, adding up to about 16 million a year. A typical thunderstorm can spill 125 million gallons of water and release enough heat to power the United States electrically for one-third of an hour. The total energy of a hurricane can exceed that of a megaton nuclear explosion.

Little appreciated, though, are "bad" weather's positive effects. Great gales—which scientists sometimes call "atmospheric air conditioners"—exchange heat for cold by blending tropical breezes with polar winds, often cleansing the air of pollutants and watering parched land. Storm-borne rain makes life possible by sustaining plants that feed the animal kingdom. Yet nature's storms, which can be exquisitely beautiful, also wield the power to kill.

KILLER STORMS

In November 1970, a cyclone in East Pakistan (now Bangladesh) flooded the coast and buried hundreds of thousands of people in mud. No accurate death toll exists, but estimates hold that 150,000 people died within hours and that starvation, disease, and exposure killed another 1 to 2 million within a few months. About 2.5 million people became homeless. The *Pakistan Observer* reported a worrisome "bad smell" among thousands of floating corpses, through which starving survivors trooped in search of food. A journalist in the Ganges delta told of 3,000 bodies littering one roadside, where survivors clambered "like mad people," howling out the names of the dead. Relief workers could barely walk through villages without stepping on bodies. Some victims were found in trees.

The Indian Ocean spawns some of Earth's

deadliest storms; these are attracted, as if magnetically, to the Bay of Bengal, where a populous, low-lying coast leaves residents exceptionally vulnerable to killer storms and floods. For example, in 1985, Bangladesh, a nation barely the size of Wisconsin with 100 million people, was hit by its sixtieth cyclone in 63 years. Massive storm surges can sweep the bay's tiny islands and shoreline. Without radios or high ground to retreat to, poverty-stricken residents in huts, many of them mud-flat farmers, have no warning and no hope.

Australia, too, has had its share of storms. In December 1974, an unwanted Christmas present arrived. Meteorologists had spotted ominous clouds in the Arafura Sea, between Australia and New Guinea, that traveled southwest toward the Indian Ocean and then blossomed into a roaring cyclone. But Australian forecasters believed it would pass 60 miles offshore. The Aussies made merry on Christmas Eve. When warnings finally went out, it was too late. At 4 A.M. on December 25, Cyclone Tracy ravaged Darwin, killing 50 people and crushing the Northern Territory capital city of 48,000.

Without doubt, storm surges and floods from tropical cyclones—the generic term for hurricanes and typhoons—cause the greatest number of fatalities in one swoop. Winds can crush buildings and flood waters can wash entire villages away. Among the world's worst storm tracks are the two that lead straight up the Bay of Bengal, affecting India and Bangladesh, and the Gulf of Mexico, grazing the United States' southern coast.

HURRICANE COUNTRY

The United States is home to some of the world's most intense atmospheric events. The deadliest have been hurricanes. In 1900, a gale that whipped Galveston, Texas, killed more than 6,000 people, leaving an additional 5,000 injured and 10,000 homeless. Rising to a memorable

blood-colored dawn on Saturday, September 8, mariners recalled the old adage: "Red sky at night, sailor's delight; red in the morning, sailor take warning." Despite the glaring red warning, however, most of the salty Texans did not bother to prepare. The booming port city of 40,000, whose numerous wharves served 1,000 ships a year, stood on a barrier island partitioning Galveston Bay from the Gulf of Mexico. Only three miles wide, with a 4.5-foot elevation, Galveston lay ominously exposed.

After a local weatherman saw his barometer plummet, he raced his horse cart along the shore, shouting about the coming storm. It was already too late. By noon, both bridges off the island were swamped. One by one, huge combers swept away beachfront homes, thrashed buildings, and raked the island clean. By nightfall,

half the city's wooden buildings had been splintered into driftwood.

Nearly a century has passed since the Galveston tragedy, and during that time no U.S. hurricane has come close to claiming so many lives. Since 1972, when Hurricane Agnes posted a death toll of 122, no storm has taken more than 95 U.S. fatalities. Credit for this goes mostly to vastly improved monitoring and forecasting methods, plus better warning and evacuation systems.

Even Camille, the second strongest category 5 hurricane in U.S. history, claimed only 256 lives when it tore up Louisiana, Mississippi, and Alabama in 1969. Measured on the Saffir-Simpson Hurricane Scale, a category 5 storm produces winds above 155 miles per hour, causes a storm surge above 18 feet, and reduces buildings to rubble. Even compared to the fiercest-ever

Above, a section of the Ben Sawyer Bridge that linked Isle of Palms, South Carolina, to the mainland was swept aside and rendered impassable on September 21, 1989, by Hurricane Hugo.

Opposite, toppled railway cars attest to the strength of Hurricane Elena, which caused approximately $1.3 billion in damage and took four lives in Florida and Louisiana in September 1985.

category 5 hurricane—which swept the Florida Keys in 1935 and killed 408 people—Camille was intense. Wielding 200-mile-per-hour gusts, the gale lumbered up the Mississippi delta at dusk on August 17 and struck New Orleans. By dark, the world's longest bridge, the 26-mile-long Pontchartrain causeway, was submerged. Near midnight, a 20-foot storm surge washed over Mississippi's coast, carrying whole buildings and their occupants inland.

Among those victims were 24 unflappable sun worshippers who, thumbing their noses at Camille, decided to stay in their beachfront Richelieu Apartments and party. Camille was not pleased. The Richelieu, in Pass Christian, Mississippi, stood dead center in the storm's path. Like a cardboard box before a roaring truck, the Richelieu was crushed out of existence. Only one person, Mary Ann Gerlach, survived. She swam out a second-story window after the storm surge broke the glass and filled her apartment with sea-water. Outside, clinging to a plank, Gerlach saw her husband drown, then watched the Richelieu cave in. Floating in high seas, she finally settled in a tree, clinging there until her rescue the next day.

UNDERSTANDING THE KILLERS

So far this century, 31 storms have killed 25 or more U.S. residents. During the past two decades, only Hurricane Andrew has been that deadly. Americans, not surprisingly, have some justification for believing that most weather-related deaths are preventable. Yet internationally, astonishing numbers of weather fatalities occur almost unnoticed on a regular basis.

Take 1993, not an unusual year, as an example. That year, fierce monsoons in southwest Asia soaked southern Nepal, where floods and landslides—the worst in a century—left 2,000 people dead and thousands more homeless. In northern India, rain-swollen rivers washed out homes and

Yacht owners survey their damaged craft, above, forcibly dry-docked on the marina's jetty by Hurricane Hugo in 1989.

Opposite, grounded ships in Gulfport, Mississippi, appear to drift in a sea of aluminum cans created by Hurricane Camille in 1969.

Right, police arrest two looters in Florida City, Florida. Rampant looting that followed Hurricane Andrew resulted in an estimated 2,500 arrests in two months.

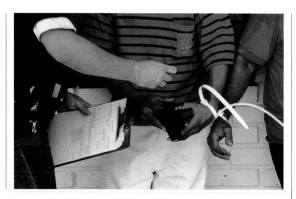

Two scenes from Homestead, Florida, following Andrew's devastation: Above, a woman displays the shotgun she uses to guard her remaining possessions at a temporary campground. Right, a stern warning to any would-be looters emblazons the side of this house.

Opposite, the wreckage of a Dadeland mobile-home park reveals the magnitude of destruction visited on Florida by Hurricane Andrew during the early-morning darkness of August 24, 1992. One of the nation's costliest natural disasters, with a price tag of more than $25 billion, Andrew destroyed or severely damaged some 80,000 homes and left a swath of devastation larger than the city of Chicago.

bridges, killing 800 people and marooning thousands. Iran saw five days of constant rain destroy 96,000 houses and claim 407 lives. Tropical Storm Bret severely flooded Colombia, Nicaragua, Costa Rica, Honduras, and Venezuela. Caracas alone lost 170 people. A month later, Tropical Storm Gert drove 15,000 Nicaraguans and Hondurans from their houses, killing 70, before attacking Mexico, where 35 people drowned while 85,000 fled their water-filled dwellings.

Those are just the fatal occurrences. In the summer of 1993, 14 tropical storms and typhoons battered Japan, destroying its rice crops. For people living in the United States, these figures numb the mind. But for most of the world, large weather catastrophes remain a painfully common part of life.

Scientists have waged a mighty war to understand these storms. The advent of satellites, parallel computers, Doppler radar, lidar (a laser-driven wind-watching system), and other sophisticated tools has driven a veritable revolution in meteorology. Still, killer storms give forecasters their worst headaches. Predictions are now fairly accurate for large-scale weather systems covering several states, and local weather, such as a town's afternoon forecast. But medium-range, or mesoscale, weather events, such as a storm front affecting one or two states and the infamous three- to five-day forecast, still leave meteorologists wringing their hands.

Yet this much they do know: when a warm, moist air mass meets a cold, dry one along a front and a low-pressure zone forms in the middle, trouble is up. Those ingredients, under the right conditions, can brew a major disaster. Earth's summertime tropics provide the right ingredients for cooking up a cyclone. Out at sea, huge masses of humid air rise off sun-baked waters into cold upper altitudes, congealing into a loose patchwork of thunderstorms serving as cyclone seedlings. Most storms dissipate. But with the

right conditions and a well-timed trigger, they can twirl into a cyclone.

In the Atlantic Ocean, that trigger is often a low-pressure wave from the African coast that moves out over open sea. In the Pacific and Indian Oceans, trade winds coupled with Earth's rotational forces can set thunderstorms spinning cyclonically. Most early storm seedlings, or tropical depressions, die out. In the Atlantic Ocean each year, only nine or 10 of the 100 or so observable tropical depressions reach storm intensities, with winds above 39 miles per hour. About five tropical storms mushroom into mature hurricanes with winds above 74 miles per hour.

Once under way, a cyclone circles a low-pressure core that intensifies as the storm grows stronger. The tubular core, or eye, remains calm, a place where exhausted dry air spills back to the sea. Around the eye a wall of wind, or eyewall, spins fastest, often above 100 miles per hour. Driven by the low-pressure center, the storm sucks humid air up from the sea, cools it, then dumps dry air and rain back down. This organized condensing of sea mist keeps a cyclone spinning, the warm sea water serving as metaphorical steam for the atmosphere's spinning turbine.

With a natural tendency to travel west, then curve either north or south, a tropical cyclone may take four to ten days to travel to Australia or into the Bay of Bengal or Gulf of Mexico. If a cyclone rides over land, its fuel supply of warm ocean moisture dries up and it tends to break down into a network of thunderstorms, often spawning tornadoes.

TORNADO TALES

Each spring, a 460-mile strip of land reaching across Missouri, Kansas, Oklahoma, and the Texas Panhandle (nicknamed Tornado Alley) attracts storm gazers from all over the world to watch its dancing funnels. The wide open spaces of the region's Big Sky set an ideal stage

for up to 300 twisters a year, more than anywhere else on Earth.

As the Gulf of Mexico's humid breezes waft north, they merge with frigid winds blowing south from Canada, forming atmospheric whirls high over the plains. When sheets of hot air rub up against sheets of cold air, they can roll up horizontally and drop down, almost like cresting tubular waves. Sometimes, they yield rotating funnel clouds, whose central swirl focuses into a twisting tube. On the ground, tornadoes move at up to 40 miles per hour, blasting everything they touch. With winds of 200 to 300 miles per hour spinning around a low-pressure core, a

These before and after shots show how Hurricane Andrew stripped Cape Florida bare. Remarkably, the 146-year-old lighthouse and nearby structures managed to withstand a storm surge nearly nine feet above sea level.

Opposite, this ibis was among the wildlife victims of Andrew's killer winds. The hurricane dealt a severe blow to the ecosystems of Florida and Louisiana, especially to the already fragile Everglades.

twister can chew up a house like a chunk of watermelon, then spit the seeds out miles away.

Their lore is legendary. Fickle twisters have blown homes apart, yet left crystal brandy snifters intact. Farm animals have been lifted, carried, and set down unharmed. In 1977, a chicken in Birmingham, Alabama, had the feathers plucked clean off its back. Small objects, like pencils and spoons, have pierced deeply into brick walls. Cars and trucks have been found flattened and crumpled into wrinkled sheets.

Twisters have also lofted objects for amazing distances. On April 18, 1955, a funnel picked up a car with two passengers in Lanark, Illinois, and ferried it 100 feet before setting it down virtually unscathed. During a major tornado outbreak on April 3, 1974, a Madison, Indiana, family sought cover in a closet, which remarkably was the only structure standing after a killer tornado leveled their home. A nearby house, crushed to rubble, had its kitchen cupboard carried away and set gently down, all dishes intact. In 1931, the express train Empire Builder, zipping through Moorhead, Minnesota, had five 83-ton coaches lifted from the tracks, then dropped; one car with 117 passengers landed 80 feet away. Following a tornado in Blue Springs, Nebraska, on September 26, 1973, a farmer found a baby grand piano in a field some 1,300 feet from its living room home.

Tornadoes' tricks seem arbitrary, but given their shape—especially so-called killer tornadoes, whose multiple vortices often dangle from the main funnel—their seemingly random paths make sense. Flailing and undulating, they grab and crush only what lies directly in the wind's way.

Among the greatest firsthand accounts of a killer tornado is that of Roy S. Hall, a retired U.S. Army captain in McKinney, Texas, whose family, trapped inside the twister, survived to tell the story in *Weatherwise* magazine.

On May 3, 1943, Captain Hall and his family watched helplessly as a giant rotating cloud, dragging an ink-black, lightning-streaked curtain of rain, descended on their home. From a window, Hall watched trees and shrubs flatten to the ground. When the tornado hovered directly overhead, all sound ceased, he said, except for a "hard pulse beat" in his head. A strange bluish light filled the room. Papers and magazines rose to the ceiling. He tried to walk, but the floor shifted beneath his feet. Loose objects "flashed upward," and he sensed that the roof had gone. Moments later, wind pulled him into the fireplace while a living room wall crumbled as if hit "by a gigantic sledge hammer." Hall clawed through debris to grab his four-year-old daughter, as the house shifted from its foundation and smashed into trees.

In silence, he saw a giant concave rim descend over his house, motionless, "save for a slow up-and-down pulsation." It was the lower end of the tornado.

"I was looking at its inside, and we were, at the moment, within the tornado itself," he exclaimed. "The interior of the funnel was hollow, the rim itself appearing to be not over 10 feet in thickness and, owing possibly to the light within the funnel, appeared perfectly opaque. Its inside was so slick and even that it resembled the interior of a glazed standpipe. The rim had another motion which I was, for a moment, too dazzled to grasp," Hall said. "The whole thing was rotating, shooting past from right to left with incredible velocity."

Dazed and confused, Hall moved to cover his daughter. "My stricken eyes beheld something few have ever seen before and lived to tell about. I was looking far up the interior of a great tornado funnel! It extended upward for over a thousand feet, and was swaying gently, and bending slowly toward the southeast. Down at the bottom, judging from the circle in front of me, the funnel was about 150 yards across. Higher up it was larger, and seemed to be partly filled with a

Left, its roots ripped from the ground, a palm tree's trunk mashes a Florida dwelling.

Above, tent cities like this one in Homestead, Florida, provided displaced residents with an orderly atmosphere and the basic necessities of life after Hurricane Andrew.

Left, a catch-as-catch-can builder stowed his shop in his car and traveled in search of jobs to the area of hurricane damage.

Opposite, evicted by Andrew, a survivor returns to the desolation of destroyed home and belongings. The superhurricane spared nearby Miami and saved its fury for the small town of Homestead, Florida.

bright cloud, which shimmered like a fluorescent light. This brilliant cloud was in the middle of the funnel, not touching the sides, as I recall having seen the walls extending on up outside the cloud.

"Up there too, where I could observe both the front and back of the funnel, the terrific whirling could be plainly seen. As the upper portion of the huge pipe swayed over, another phenomenon took place. It looked as if the whole column were composed of rings or layers, and when a higher ring moved on toward the southeast, the ring immediately below slipped over to get back under it. This rippling motion continued on down toward the lower tip.

"If there was any debris in the wall of the funnel, it was whirling so fast I could not see it. And if there was a vacuum inside the funnel, as is commonly believed, I was not aware of it. I do not recall having any difficulty breathing, nor did I see any debris rushing up under the rim of the tornado, as there surely would have been had there been a vacuum. I am positive that the shell of the twister was not composed of wreckage, dirt, or other debris. Air, it must have been, thrown out into a hollow tube by centrifugal force. But if this is true, why was there no vacuum, and why was the wall opaque?

"When the wave-like motion reached the lower tip, the far edge of the funnel was forced downward and jerked toward the southeast. This edge, in passing, touched the roof of my neighbor's house and flicked the building away like a flash of light. Where, an instant before, had stood a recently constructed home, now remained one small room with no roof. The house, as a whole, did not resist the tornado for the fractional part of a second. When the funnel touched it, the building dissolved, the various parts shooting off to the left like sparks from an emery wheel.

"The very instant the rim of the funnel passed

beyond the wreck of the house, long vaporous-appearing streamers, pale blue in color, extended out and upward toward the southeast from each corner of the remaining room. They appeared to be about 20 feet long and six inches wide, and after hanging perfectly stationary for a long moment, were suddenly gone.

"The peculiar bluish light was now fading and was gone abruptly. Instantly it was again dark as night. With the darkness my hearing began to come back. I could hear the excited voices of my family in the small back room, six feet away, and the crunching jars of heavy objects falling around the house. The tornado had passed."

ANATOMY OF A TWISTER

In the United States alone about 800 twisters touch down each year, killing 80 people and injuring 1,500. The Southeast sees by far the most tornadoes, which form mainly from March to June, peaking in April and May. As warm, moist breezes collide with cold, dry winds, funnels can form but remain invisible until they pick up dirt and take on color, or sweep up water and create elegant waterspouts. A twister may never touch down, or it may cut a long, wide swath. Since tornadoes vary in width from a few dozen to several hundred yards, they can leave mile-wide trails more than 200 miles long, though the average path runs 16 miles. On May 26, 1917, for example, a tornado took seven hours and 20 minutes to traverse 293 miles through Illinois and Indiana. Owing to southerly wind currents, tornadoes usually move toward the northeast along with the thunderstorms spawning them.

The swiftness with which tornadoes arise, do their damage, and vanish makes them lurid, fearsome, and mysterious. They strike "like vampires in the night," says one forecaster. In fact, most tornadoes occur during early evening, the warmest part of a day. Some 82 percent of

Above, a tornado's rotating terror is fueled by updrafts in a thunderstorm. Winds in the anvil top of the vicious cloud cause the twister to travel cross-country, often in unpredictable paths.

Left, a dreaded funnel silhouette slips from the wall cloud at the base of a thunderstorm, marking the birth of a twister.

Opposite, mammatus clouds often herald the onset of a tornado. Anyone observing such a formation is advised to seek safety at once.

all tornadoes strike between noon and midnight, with 23 percent occurring from 4 P.M. to 6 P.M. A typical warm day's weather cycle sees humidity rise all morning, chill into clouds after noon, then build into thunderstorms in late afternoon or early evening.

Inside the anvil of a thundercloud, condensing water and electrical activity thin out its center, creating a low-pressure area that pulls in air from its underside. Sometimes a low-hanging mound called a mammatus appears, often alongside heavy, greenish rain and large hailstones. Updrafts spin into the cloud's core. This action opens a funnel that appears to drop down and ripen in color when it meets earth.

As the tornado tightens, it speeds up and becomes more dangerous. The effect is much like a twirling skater pulling in her arms to increase rotation. An innocent five-mile-per-hour breeze circling an object four miles away has enough energy to tighten into a tornado with 160-mile-per-hour winds. Scientists believe that twister winds reach around 300 miles per hour, an extraordinary intensity. Since a wind's power increases by the square of its speed, a 300-mile-per-hour wind packs 100 times, not 10 times, the punch of a 30-mile-per-hour gust. Thus little eddies at a tornado's edge—often spinning into tentacle-like suction vortices near the ground—can cut through homes almost like a circular saw buzzing through plywood.

Cloud systems organize and focus a tornado's energies. The white, puffy cumulus clouds that swell at 2,000 to 5,000 feet eventually build into cumulonimbus clouds, which stand out ominously like towering, black giants. Rising above 35,000 feet, airborne ice crystals coalesce into a loose cloud network. When heavy enough, the ice tumbles down, melting into rain and dragging cool downdrafts of air.

When updrafts come fast enough to offset falling ice and rain, hailstones form. The frozen raindrops thicken in onionlike layers until updrafts can no longer keep them aloft. Eventually icy lumps, sometimes as large as baseballs or grapefruits, come crashing down. (The largest known hailstone was a 5.5-inch glob weighing 1.67 pounds that crashed in Coffeyville, Kansas, in 1970.) The bigger the hailstones, the faster the updraft supporting them, which is why big hailstones often precede killer tornadoes. Hail rarely kills, though on May 22, 1986, an unusual monster hailstorm over China's Sichuan Province left 9,000 people injured and 100 dead.

With downdrafts and hail, a potentially violent storm is under way. Simultaneous updraft-downdraft pairs, called cells, may network, fuel each other, and form supercells or squall lines. Whereas a normal thunderstorm lasts about 40 minutes, a supercell goes on for hours, can travel hundreds of miles, and often spits out tornadoes.

About two out of three twisters are considered "weak," lasting less than ten minutes with winds below 110 miles per hour. "Strong" tornadoes last about 20 minutes and wield gusts between 110 and 205 miles per hour; they account for 30 percent of deaths from tornadoes. But the most vicious of all twisters, the "killer" tornadoes, really keep forecasters jumping. Although only 2 percent of all tornadoes, they account for 70 percent of tornado deaths, with winds above 205 miles per hour spinning for more than an hour.

Trying to grasp how such killer storms form, Howard Bluestein and his band of tornado chasers from the University of Oklahoma, Norman, have, since 1977, run toward tornadoes while others run away. Bluestein listens for severe storm warnings, then hightails over to a safe spot where he captures data on the rotating funnels with a portable Doppler radar. In the early 1980s, his team used to heave a 400-pound Totable Tornado Observatory, nicknamed TOTO, into the paths of oncoming tornadoes—

Above, wood splinters and bricks burst when a two-by-four timber is shot from a cannon into a masonry wall to simulate the force of a tornado. When such flying fragments cause other structures to disintegrate, more and more projectiles—including flying metal—fill the air, and a deadly chain reaction occurs.

Opposite, sequential exposures follow a tornado as it rips across the Great Plains. Pictures are viewed from left to right, top to bottom. Debris is lifted from the ground, then flung outward after first being wrapped around the funnel and spun at express-train speeds. Dirt, stones, and other projectiles often remain outside the funnel, instead of being sucked up through its narrow tip as with a vacuum cleaner nozzle.

Pages 46-47: When this Cheyenne, Wyoming, tornado ripped apart the Shannon Heights mobile-home park on July 16, 1979, Peter Willing clicked off shots as long as he dared, then dived for the relative safety of his basement. The disaster destroyed 17 trailers and killed a small child.

though they quit using the device when better methods became available.

Studying tornadoes by decoding their footprints, Tetsuya Fujita at the University of Chicago—calling himself a detective who tracks tornado crimes—has examined more than 2,000 miles of trails left by twisters. In 1971, based on his observations, he invented the Fujita Wind Damage Scale, which correlates a tornado's wind speed with its destructive power. A tornado with an F-1 rating, for instance, wields winds of 73 to 112 miles per hour and blows out windows and roofs; an F-5 tornado, with winds of 261 to 318 miles per hour, first explodes buildings, then flings the debris away.

Fujita made some startling observations after one of the worst tornado outbreaks in history. On Wednesday, April 3, 1974, forecasters noticed a monster cold front moving eastward at 35 miles per hour from the Rocky Mountains. Hanging over the southern coastal states that day was an unstable mass of tropical air. The two fronts met, tumbling into storms that spanned Louisiana, Tennessee, and Kentucky. Just after noon, three nasty squall lines emerged. One reached from Lake Michigan down through Illinois and Missouri; a second, from Indiana across Kentucky and Tennessee; a third appeared in Georgia and Alabama. Satellites showed giant thunderheads topping 60,000 feet, an ominous sign.

The first twister touched down near Morris, Illinois, at 1:10 P.M. but did no damage. An hour later, though, the hellraisers began to arrive. During a span of just over 16 hours, 148 tornadoes whipped through 13 states, killed 315 people, injured 5,484 others, and damaged more than a half-billion dollars in property. Tornado trails totaled 2,598 miles, with a mean length of 18.7 miles. Of the twisters, six earned F-5 rankings, among the most vicious ever recorded. Of the cities and towns stricken, six suffered a rare double strike.

Immediately, Fujita was at the scene. To his surprise, he found tornado paths riding up and down bumpy landscapes, as in Georgia, where one tornado climbed a 3,000-foot ridge, slid down into a 1,000-foot canyon, then crept up the opposite side to 3,300 feet, a rare path.

Flying over the twister trails, Fujita had a flashback. In 1945, as a young physicist in Japan, he had examined strange starburst-shaped ground patterns created by the atomic blast at Hiroshima. In the 1974 storm paths, he saw similar starburst shapes. This astute observation led to his controversial theory, now confirmed, that rare downbursts of air can occur in frontal storms, possibly influencing tornado outbreaks. Forecasters often compare the 1974 tornado episodes to the fearsome Palm Sunday Outbreak on April 11, 1965, when 37 twisters killed 271 Midwesterners and injured more than 5,000 in one day.

Though spring yields more tornado peril than any other season, tornadoes can develop at any time, in any U.S. state—a theme painfully proved by the Thanksgiving tornado disaster of 1992. Starting in early afternoon on Saturday, November 21, 94 twisters tortured 13 states for 48 hours. Rankin County, Mississippi, suffered the first fatalities on Saturday night, when an F-4 twister tore up a mobile-home park, then crushed a two-story brick home. The twisters tracked as far north as Indiana and Ohio, with four touching down in Virginia and Maryland. In the end, investigators found 26 dead, 641 injured, and $291 million in damages.

Searching for a silver lining in the disaster, some forecasters see the 1992 figures as a victory for safety: the twisters claimed less than 8 percent of the 1974 deaths. A Disaster Survey Team credited a new network of Doppler radars and a streamlined warning system for the vastly reduced number of fatalities. In Houston, Texas, for example, warnings preceded 15 of 17

Above, carefully contrived fumes and drafts call forth a phantom twister. In such vortex chambers, researchers spawn working models of the weather. Joined with facts gained from work in the field, such academic exercises provide data for computer modelers.

Top, the glowing computer projects virtual reality for a weather scientist. He obtains a 3-D impression of forces at work within a real-life tornado.

tornado events by an unprecedented average of 25 minutes.

Advanced warning has now proven its value on an international scale. In May 1994, a newly created Space Research and Remote Sensing system, set up by the World Meteorological Organization, alerted Bangladesh to a coming cyclone. Radio broadcasts to 10,000 villages a day and a half before the cyclone struck gave residents enough time to flee the storm's 180-mile-per-hour winds and 20-foot surge. Fewer than 500 people died, compared to 130,000 deaths from a similar cyclone in 1991.

IT LOOKED LIKE HIROSHIMA

In agonizing contrast, those who receive little or no warning have only a random chance of surviving a killer tornado. Consider the tragic tale of the west Texas town of Saragosa, where, on May 22, 1987, the sun was just setting on the mostly Spanish-speaking community of 350 people. Many residents were eating supper at home. Others sat proudly in Saragosa Hall, the community center, celebrating the Head Start kindergarten graduation of 20 gleeful five-year-olds.

About 50 miles to the northeast, however, in the National Weather Service office in Midland, Texas, John V. Wright and his forecasting team were worried. Throughout the day the skies had tumbled ferociously, with reports of monster thunderclouds and hail. In midafternoon Wright's team had issued severe thunderstorm advisories and urged emergency managers to stay alert. Each hour since brought worsening conditions. By dusk, no one knew what to expect.

The Sky Warn network—a group of 40 ham radio operators trained as storm spotters—scanned the clouds. At 7 P.M., a Sky Warn alert from schoolteacher Glenn Humphreys noted that "the clouds are moving in different directions and altitudes and seem to be building

Scientists erect TOTO, short for Totable Tornado Observatory, in the path of a twister. The scientists then quickly scurry out of harm's way. As the funnel cloud strikes, their mechanical "Wizard of Oz" records its pulse and other vital statistics.

without moving off. They look very restless." They were also, Humphreys calculated, ominous: "The sky looks wicked and full of energy, but down here it's deathly still."

Within half an hour, Weather Service radar had picked up a severe thunderstorm 63,000 feet high and 15 miles northwest of Saragosa. John Wright later recalled that he immediately "issued a severe thunderstorm and flash flood warning for the county, stressing that the weather was deteriorating rapidly." At 7:46, storm spotter Charles Towry radioed that a rotating wall cloud, which usually precedes a tornado, was riding over Interstate 10 just west of Balmorhea, Texas. Two minutes later, Humphreys reported that it was "heading straight for Saragosa at 30 miles an hour."

Glued to his radar screen, Wright ordered a tornado warning for south-central Reeves County. "Everything was in chaos," Wright remembers, "but at 7:54 we finally got the thing out." Describing the storm as "extremely dangerous," the warning called for immediate tornado safety measures. Calls went out to the county sheriff's office and to the Emergency Operating Center in Pecos, 30 miles north of Saragosa, urging quick action. Sky Warn spotters confirmed the storm's path, adding reports of golf ball-sized hail. "At that point," said Wright, "we had no idea what was going to happen." Several towns in addition to Saragosa seemed to be in jeopardy.

By 8:01, warnings blared on local television sets, and someone drove through town honking a horn for attention. West of Saragosa, along Route 17, Humphreys was riding with Deputy Sheriff Floyd Estrada when they saw a rotating wall cloud overhead. They raced toward Saragosa through fierce rain and wind, their car swerving wildly as the funnel cloud passed overhead. From three miles away, state trooper Bob Bourland used the Sky Warn network to report that "a funnel is crossing the interstate." Cars and trucks began parking beneath an Interstate 10 overpass, and inside them Humphreys saw faces that were "scared, grim, awestruck."

The kindergarten graduation ceremony had begun promptly at 7:30. "That was the problem," Wright recalled. "Our warning didn't go out until 7:54, and those people were inside, totally disconnected from the outside world." Except for one father. Delayed by car trouble, he didn't arrive until 8:12 P.M. Turning into the center, he spotted an approaching twister in the rearview mirror. "Tornado!" he shouted, running inside, pulling kids offstage. Some people went outside to look and one person escaped in his car, but most of the others returned to the hall.

"I yelled for everyone to stand against the walls, but some men were already pushing tables there and putting children under them," said Elia Estrada, the deputy sheriff's wife. "Then it started to rain real hard, and the windows blew out. Rain and broken glass were flying around. The walls began to break and the roof caved in, and hail was coming down on top of us."

Lightning chasers, above, prepare to project wires into high-tension thunderheads at South Baldy, New Mexico. These latter-day Ben Franklins launch rockets, rather than kites, into electrified clouds. A wire reels out from each rocket and conducts Jovian bolts to earth.

Opposite, Arizona horizons sizzle as storm clouds invade the Tucson area.

At 8:16, all electric clocks in Saragosa stopped. Along Route 17, power lines draped the road. Estrada and Humphreys maneuvered their car under one, then realized only darkness lay before them. No lights, houses, or buildings. Estrada wondered if they were actually in Saragosa. Humphreys saw a tornado pulling away from what used to be Main Street. The two stepped from the car and gazed upon the remains of the community center.

"I couldn't see any other buildings," Humphreys remembers. "A gritty mist was whipping in our faces. It was cold, and we were soaking wet. A woman was pushing little kids into Floyd's patrol car." Humphreys radioed for help, while Elia Estrada cared for the soaked, scared, and muddied children, all with "haunted looks on their faces."

In a matter of only a few minutes, the multiple-vortex "killer" tornado, wielding three funnels, killed 31 people and injured 121 others. Damage to 87 houses, 23 mobile homes, 7 businesses, a church, and the community center totaled $8.7 million. The half-mile-wide tornado cut a three-mile-long swath through Saragosa's middle. Of the 80 persons attending the graduation, 22 perished. "Amazingly, all of the kids survived, though I can't imagine how. It must have been a miracle," said Wright. "Seeing what was left of that building, it's hard to believe anyone survived. They only had 90 seconds of warning." Ironically, Wright believes that the graduation saved many lives by sheltering people in the town's most solid structure. "Without that ceremony, most would have been at home, without a chance."

For the rest of that night, emergency volunteers struggled to free survivors from rubble. Humphreys radioed ambulances, monitored Sky Warn, and coordinated civil defense. At the weather office, tension remained high, and Wright tracked yet another wall cloud perilously

Top, near Florida's Kennedy Space Center, summoned lightning travels down a copper wire, trailing behind a rocket launched into a storm cloud over Mosquito Lagoon.

Above, Debbie Prell of the Langmuir Laboratory for Atmospheric Research in New Mexico prepares wire-trailing rockets to trigger lightning strikes in 1992.

Opposite, Federal Express control tower in Memphis, Tennessee, guides aircraft with help from the National Lightning Detection Network. On average, commercial jets are hit once a year each by lightning, with little damage.

Pages 54-55: Deliberately set, a small
grass fire at Tallgrass Prairie Preserve,
Oklahoma, helps prevent larger blazes in
the future. Since 1972, the National
Park Service has recognized that fire is
part of the natural cycle of the land.

Right, smoke billows high above
Wyoming's Yellowstone National Park
in 1988.

Above, a Boeing Vertol Chinook helicopter assists firefighters. Destruction
advanced as far as 14 miles a day in the
1988 Yellowstone fires.

Opposite, during the summer and fall
of 1988, a forest inferno raged through
Yellowstone burning 160,000 acres.

close to Saragosa. The "totality of the destruction" struck Wright the hardest. "Where once
there had been a school, a hotel, a depot, suddenly there was nothing. It was inconceivable
that so much could be wiped out so quickly and
so completely. Nothing was left standing.
It looked like Hiroshima after the war."

INSIDE NATURE'S BEDLAM

Scientists have had a hard time seeing the inner
workings of monster storms, whose tumultuous,
electrically active interiors make penetrations difficult, unless they happen by accident.

Late on the sunny afternoon of July 26, 1959,
Marine Lieutenant Colonel William H. Rankin
strapped himself into an F8U Crusader jet fighter
and cranked up its engine for what promised to
be a routine 600-mile flight from Massachusetts
to North Carolina. The World War II veteran
didn't think much about his flight, even when a
local forecaster warned of possible thunderstorms near Norfolk, Virginia. The report set the
storms near 40,000 feet. So Rankin decided simply to soar over them at 50,000 feet.

He had a clean flight down to Norfolk, where
at about 6 P.M. he caught a glimpse of the predicted storm, its mounting black thunderhead brewing somewhat higher than anticipated. He continued to climb, still aiming to fly over the roiling
cloud mass. But a flashing red light changed his
plans. Rankin's engines rumbled, the fire-warning
light blinked, and his power failed. The engine
had seized. For about 20 seconds, he considered

Pages 58-59: The Mississippi River floods farmlands near St. Louis during the summer of 1993.

Right, a boater paddles into a local store in Portage des Sioux, Missouri, during July 1993. "It's like Venice," said a Coast Guard officer. A tornado touched down here at the height of the flooding.

Above, water laps at the seats of a stadium in Davenport, Iowa, in April 1993.

Opposite, on August 1, 1993, more than 8 million gallons of water per second flowed past the Gateway Arch in St. Louis, Missouri. Flood damage was estimated at between $10 and $15 billion.

his options, while his plane plummeted.

At 47,000 feet, Rankin made the critical decision to eject. "I had never heard of anyone's having ejected at that altitude," Rankin later said. "The temperature outside was close to 70 degrees below zero. I had on only a summer-weight flying suit, gloves, helmet, and Marine field shoes." Falling through the frigid winds at 10,000 feet per minute, Rankin first felt a stinging cold, then "a blessed numbness." Decompression from the high altitude's thin air stretched and distended his abdomen until he "thought it would burst." His eyes felt as if "they were being ripped from their sockets," his head as if it were "splitting,"

his ears "bursting inside," and his body "racked by cramps."

At a lower altitude inside the cloud, air pressure increased, easing his pain. Dazed and numb, Rankin saw his parachute open automatically. About to relax, hoping he was finally home free, he was suddenly smacked by a frigid air blast, jarring him "from head to toe." Deep into the storm's roiling winds, he soared "up and up and up." Soon he plummeted again, finding himself inside "an angry ocean of boiling clouds—blacks and grays and whites, spilling over one another, into one another, digesting one another.

"I became a molecule trapped in the thermal pattern of the heat engine, buffeted in all directions—up, down, sideways, clockwise, counterclockwise, over and over. I zoomed straight up, straight down, feeling all the weird sensations of G forces—positive, negative, and zero. I was stretched, slammed, and pounded. I was a bag of flesh and bones crashing into a concrete floor."

After being "shot up like a shell leaving a cannon," Rankin said, "I found myself looking down into a long, black tunnel... This was nature's bedlam, a black cageful of screaming lunatics, beating me with big flat sticks, roaring at me, trying to crush me. All this time it had been raining so torrentially that I thought I would drown in midair. Several times I had held my breath, fearing to inhale quarts of water."

Finally emerging from the storm, Rankin crashed into a tree. Dizzy, confused, he wondered what time it was, knowing he had ejected at 6 P.M. His wristwatch read 6:40 P.M.

LIGHTING THE HEAVENS

Rankin was lucky. Despite injuries from decompression, which stretched, sprained, and lacerated his body—it even pressed his flight suit's

Missourians kept their sense of humor, right, as this sign on a building in St. Louis shows. Unfortunately, many business owners had such confidence in the protection of local levees that they had failed to buy flood insurance.

Above, downtown Davenport, Iowa, in July 1993. The entire state of Iowa was declared a federal disaster area from June through August.

Right, soggy victims of the flood of 1993. The Mississippi and Missouri Rivers ravaged 15,600 square miles, damaged 55,000 homes, and killed 50 people.

stitch marks into his flesh—he survived to fly again. Miraculously, he was not hit by lightning as he plummeted through the cloud's potentially deadly electric field.

Giant bolts from monster storms kill on average 70 to 80 people in the United States each year. In fact, at any given moment around the globe, storms collectively spark some 100 flashes a second, totaling about 8.6 million a day. Earth and the atmosphere constantly exchange charges to keep an overall balance, and storms play a big role in the process.

For reasons that scientists still do not completely understand, storm clouds separate charges into positive and negative clusters. Negative charges settle mostly in a cloud's underbelly, where they build up giant voltages. As the cloud blows along, a positively charged electrical shadow, caused by the negative pull overhead, may form on the land below.

Then comes the flash. An electrical channel forms, perhaps five miles long yet only as thick as a pen, and in a few thousandths of a second, current flows at 466 million feet per second.

So fast does lightning strike that its many steps appear as one seamless stroke. But the smoothness is an illusion. In a bolt's first one-hundredth of a second, a stepped leader reaches down about 100 feet just under a cloud, pauses, then lurches earthward. Nearing the ground, it attracts a streamer of positive charges welling up from a high point, such as a tree. The positive charges leap up, meet the negative ones, and complete a circuit about 50 yards above the ground. Next comes the upward return stroke. Driven by 100 million volts of electrical potential, up to 20,000 amperes of positive current flow skyward at one-third the speed of light, heating the channel to 50,000 degrees Fahrenheit, five times hotter than the Sun's surface. The return stroke creates light. Heated air along the channel expands violently, creating thunder,

THE JOHNSTOWN FLOOD

A house skewered by a tree was among the tragic sights of Johnstown's Main Street after the flood of May 1889.

The deadliest flood in U.S. history broke loose on Friday, May 31, 1889, in Johnstown, Pennsylvania, on Memorial Day weekend.

The quaint manufacturing city of 30,000 lay nestled in a narrow river valley between Pittsburgh and Altoona, along the Pennsylvania Railroad's main line. When an estimated six to nine inches of rain poured into the Conemaugh River basin, the river jumped its banks. By late morning, water was rushing into factories, stores, and homes.

Fifteen miles upstream a two-mile-long reservoir called Lake Conemaugh was overriding its earthen dam. Originally built as part of a canal project in the early 1850s, the lake had for a decade been a private fishing camp for wealthy sportsmen and their families. The dam measured about 900 feet wide by 70 feet high and had been in poor condition for some time. It towered more than 400 feet above the City of Johnstown.

About 3:10 P.M., in the words of the Reverend G. W. Brown, who watched achingly from a hillside, "the dam melted away." Brown said a wall of water roared through the valley with a "rush that made the hills quake." It hit the city an hour later.

The liquid avalanche advanced at 20 to 40 miles an hour, scoured a three-block-wide swath of devastation and stripped the valley clean. When the water finally stilled, a 30-acre stew of wreckage—telephone poles, houses, railroad tracks and even trains—rested against Johnstown's stone bridge. The debris also contained hundreds of trapped survivors, many of whom who were burned alive when the wreckage caught fire. The final death toll was 2,209, approximating the loss of life caused by the 1906 San Francisco earthquake. ■

whose sound waves creep along at 720 miles per hour.

Sometimes a single bolt will strike. Other times, lightning storms ensue. On a Sunday afternoon in February 1987, storm watchers in Biloxi, Mississippi, on the Gulf of Mexico, watched as 458 lightning bolts tore through the air. The display was part of a grand mesoscale system—with electric veins lacing its roiling skies—that stretched over 150 miles and took 24 hours to traverse Florida to the Atlantic. By midnight, over Gainesville, Florida, its electrical ferocity peaked at 700 flashes an hour.

Like tornadoes, lightning has been known to play freakish tricks, melting holes in church bells, welding chains into iron bars, cooking potatoes in the field, and blasting wooden sailboat masts into shavings. Attracted to tall metal objects, lightning has electrified people swinging golf clubs, holding umbrellas or radio antennas, even talking on the phone. Jolted telephone poles can send current along wires into a phone user's hands, killing three or four people each year.

Lightning also starts fires. In hot, dry climates, a random strike into sun-dried fields or trees can ignite a blaze that may roar out of control. In 1991, in Oakland, California, 24 people died in freak fires that charred $1.2 billion in property.

Still, no scene shows a forest fire's ravages better than the one in Yellowstone National Park in the fall of 1988, after reportedly benign blazes flared into a fearsome firestorm. In the end, 1.4 million acres lay scorched. Where pine trees once graced green hills, whole vistas came to resemble lunar landscapes with ashen plains pocked by charcoal posts. In the worst conflagration in 200 years, eight distinct fires joined forces to fuel a Dantean inferno, with steel-melting heat and flames that jumped roads and rivers, exploded boulders, and drove tornadic winds.

Above, too wet even for frogs, a levee in West Alton, Missouri, holds amphibian survivors. Wedged between the Missouri and Mississippi Rivers, the town and a third of St. Charles County vanished as the confluence moved 20 miles farther north.

Top, a woman in Quincy, Illinois, during July 1993 exhibits defiance in the face of rising floodwaters.

The Missouri River rages over a highway on the outskirts of Hermann, Missouri, opposite, in 1993. Here, on March 5, the river rose 11 feet in 48 hours.

An innocent 1972 policy decision had also inadvertently fanned the flames. The National Park Service had decided to let small fires run their natural course, fostering their ecological role as clearers of dead brush and poppers of pine cones, which spill new seeds when heated. At the time, the policy made sense.

But Park officials began to worry as they saw Yellowstone devoured by flames, which caught them off guard. A major drought, coupled with a mountain pine beetle plague that had killed half the trees several years earlier, had turned the Park's dead lodgepole pines into the equivalent of kiln-dried kindling. Since there had been few small fires in recent years to burn up the organic debris, the forests had grown chock-full of firewood.

Heat and drought were not unique to Yellowstone; the dry spell set off blazes nation-wide from Minnesota to California in 1988. By summer's end, the United States had lost 3.7 million acres in the 48 contiguous states, plus 2 million more acres in Alaska. Some 30,000 firefighters had battled 70,000 blazes, costing about $600 million.

On July 21, with 16,600 acres burning, Yellowstone officials changed their minds and chose to suppress the fires. But by then it was too late. With steady winds and no rain, suppression efforts failed. On August 20, the park's grimmest day, 62,000 acres were ablaze; including neighboring acreage, 160,000. In contrast, only 146,000 Yellowstone acres had burned in the preceding 116 years.

By September 7, nearly 10,000 civilian and military firefighters had invaded park grounds. They slashed trees, cleared land, and soaked the Old Faithful Inn. Completed in 1904, the world's largest log building found itself nearly surrounded by hungry flames fanned by 50-mile-per-hour gusts. Flying over an orange and black wall of fire and smoke, aircraft unloaded fire-suppressing chemicals. Then the wind shifted, carrying heat

Above, volunteers in Des Moines, Iowa, struggle to build a levee. On July 11, 1993, the Des Moines River more than doubled its original flood stage of 12 feet.

Opposite, a Clarksville, Missouri, farmer uses his crops to send a message of helplessness in the face of impending disaster brought on by the Mississippi floods of 1993.

Above, a farmer in Des Moines, Iowa, looks over his harvest, submerged in floodwaters from the Des Moines River. Crop losses alone from the 1993 deluge exceeded $5 billion.

Opposite, Randolph County Sheriff Ben Picou wrestles stranded pigs from the roof of a barn as the Mississippi engulfs Kaskaskia Island, Illinois. Said Picou, "I must have hugged about 300 hogs on Kaskaskia that day."

away from the Inn's water-soaked wood. In the end, the Inn survived, though 24 nearby structures turned to char.

Eventually, the Yellowstone calamity roared itself into submission. September rains and snow gradually soothed the burning beast, though fires smoldered into November. In its wake, scattered among burnt fields, lay millions of lodgepole pine seed wings, which ecologists estimated could spawn 5,800 new trees per acre.

TAMING LAWLESS STREAMS

The alternation of droughts and floods has proved a familiar American phenomenon. Whereas in 1988 searing heat baked the Midwest, leading to the deaths of an estimated 5,000 to 10,000 people, by 1993 those same parched plains lay waterlogged, soaked by the overflow of the Mississippi and Missouri Rivers.

The summer of 1993 saw the worst midwestern flood in U.S. history. By early August, some 15,600 square miles of land in nine states lay totally submerged, an area larger than that of Lake Erie. In some areas, homes and businesses stood in two stories of water. Even individuals accustomed to floods were astonished. River specialists predicted in July that the Mississippi would top out at 40 feet, but on August 1 at St. Louis it crested above 49 feet, 19 feet above flood stage. At the flood's peak, more than 8 million gallons of water flowed past the city's Gateway Arch every second.

In July and August, swelling rivers filled homes to the rafters, peeled concrete off roadbeds, and poured into one business district only hours after forecasters said it was safe. Churches, prisons, airports, and schools succumbed to the flowing, muddy soup. In one gothic catastrophe, hundreds of caskets rose from their graves and floated out of cemeteries. By September, 55,000 homes were sunk deep in mud; 50 people had died; 30,000 people had

Right, a surprising statement of confidence, spelled out with sandbags, marks Marty Sontheimer's home in St. Charles, Missouri.

Below, two Amana, Iowa, youngsters make the most of a murky situation as they fish off their front porch in floodwaters from the Des Moines River.

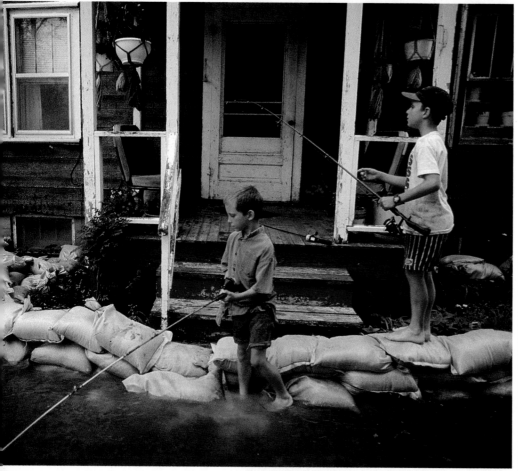

An evacuated mobile-home park, right, surrounded by Mississippi floodwaters, appears in eerie isolation. The 1993 floods damaged or destroyed more than 55,000 homes throughout the Midwest.

Opposite, surrounded by sandbags and frantically pumping water from their home, the Brake family of Ste. Genevieve, Missouri, braces for the worst.

seen their businesses wrecked. Surveyors estimated damage at $10 billion to $15 billion.

The initial creep of caramel-colored water took place over many weeks. Eight months of unusually heavy rains had saturated the earth and filled diverting flood zones and reservoirs. But the rains kept on coming. And the levees kept giving way. Tens of thousands of civilian and military volunteers frantically piled sandbags for weeks to reinforce levees. In the end, few held. In Prairie du Rocher, Illinois, proudly known as the state's oldest continuous town, residents broke one side levee to relieve pressure, a desperate act that saved the hamlet. In Hannibal, Missouri, Mark Twain's old haunt, a barrier did keep the downtown dry.

Ironically, Twain himself wrote in *Life on the Mississippi* that "one who knows the Mississippi will promptly aver...that ten thousand River Commissions, with the mines of the world at their back, cannot tame that lawless stream, cannot curb it or confine it, cannot say to it, 'Go here,' or 'Go there,' and make it obey."

Despite Twain's prescient words, the U.S. Army Corps of Engineers forged on in 1928 with the Mississippi River and Tributaries Project, a vast network of dams and levees aimed at taming the mighty floodprone waterway.

With a natural tendency to ebb and wane, the river has supplied Midwest farmers with silt-rich soil for generations, serving the U.S. economy well. The federal government poured up to $1.36 billion a year into the region in the form of concrete river walls, some towering 36 feet above the flow.

But the project has proved to be a mixed blessing. While successfully warding off other huge floods, as it did in 1973 and 1983, it has given farmers and families a false sense of security, encouraging them to dwell on otherwise unsafe lands. Squeezing the river with concrete walls forces water to well up in tributaries and

speeds up its narrowed central flow. So long as the river runs tame, there is no problem; but an overfilled Mississippi can bleed into fields or spill over onto nearby homes.

Frustrated by its 200-year-old tussle with the headstrong river, the federal government issued a report in May 1994, urging the Corps of Engineers to give up its preference for dams and flood control and instead evacuate flood plains, relocate farms and businesses, and restore the natural flood cycle. Indicating a historic policy reversal, one conservationist told the *New York Times*: "This is like asking Mahatma Gandhi to take up arms."

Like the tides, floods come and go periodically, promoting a natural cycle of land fertilization and renewal. But not all flooding is cyclical. Flash floods, for example, pose a deadly hazard. They occur when dams or levees fail, when an ice jam gives way in a river, or when rapid rainfall over a large area pours into a narrow, lowland region. Within minutes, a valley or arroyo can fill with rainwater. Those waters can rush together into rapids that can roll boulders, tear up trees and homes, and trigger mud slides. As little as six inches of fast-moving water can knock people off their feet; a two-foot stream can sweep vehicles away. Storm waters, pouring into rivers and causing flash floods, kill more people each year than any other weather event, averaging 146 deaths annually.

Flash floods have produced some gruesome catastrophes. On June 9, 1972, in Rapid City, South Dakota, 15 inches of rain in five hours left 238 fatalities. On June 19, 1990, in Shadyside, Ohio, four inches of rain in only two hours rushed into a 30-foot-high wall of water that took 26 lives. Rain can come on fast. In Holt, Missouri, a record one foot of rain fell in 42 minutes in June 1947. In D'Hanis, Texas, a record 22 inches fell in two hours and 45 minutes in May 1935. The all-time whopper, though, took

When Mississippi floodwaters cut off the Memorial and Bayview Bridges to Missouri at Quincy, Illinois, above, local officials organized helicopter and airplane service to link the two states.

Opposite, a young man in Portage des Sioux, Missouri, saves what little he can of his possessions. Floods of 1993 drove more than 85,000 Midwesterners from their homes.

place in Muduocaidang, Nei Mongol, China, where 10 hours of rain pooled 55 inches on August 1, 1977.

In Big Thompson Canyon near Estes Park, Colorado, a deadly flash flood surprised more than 3,000 people celebrating the state's 100th anniversary on July 31, 1976. Between six and nine o'clock, a thunderstorm dumped a foot of rain into the Big Thompson River. Where at 6 P.M. the river had carried 137 cubic feet of water per second, it surged at 9 P.M. with 31,200 cubic feet, sweeping away inhabited homes and 197 cars, many filled with passengers. In the Canyon's Narrows, a 19-foot wall of water swept by with car parts, house chunks, and hissing propane tanks. In three hours, 139 people drowned, 6 others vanished, 418 homes were destroyed, and 138 dwellings were damaged.

BATTERED BY BLIZZARDS

When a water-rich airmass meets a blast of cold air, another type of monster storm, the blizzard, follows. Sending glee into the hearts of skiers and fear into the hearts of the highway patrol, great snowstorms strand and freeze their victims, who may start off hypnotized by the white flakes' gentle beauty before realizing they are trapped without heat. The Blizzard of 1888 reigns supreme in American folklore. At the time of its passage over the northeast coast from the Chesapeake Bay to Maine on Monday, March 12, forecasters had little concern.

In New York City, then considered a weather-savvy metropolis, the U.S. Signal Service warned of brisk winds and rain on Sunday before snow began to fall. Yet what arrived bore no resemblance to what they had expected. By 5:30 P.M. Monday, 21 inches of snow had buried Central Park. Albany recorded nearly 47 inches, Saratoga Springs 50 inches, and Troy an amazing 55 inches, all in a few hours.

Above, as temperatures approach freezing, Plant City, Florida, farmers turn on their sprinklers and encase their fruit in ice. The process helps save the fruit from frostbite. These orange trees, left, and strawberries, opposite, were covered on February 25, 1989, when a hard freeze destroyed about 30 percent of that state's $1.4 billion citrus crop.

Totally unprepared, New York City was devastated. Live electric wires dangled from ice-encrusted poles, some of which fell across streets. Dead horses lay beneath snow drifts. Four elevated train lines froze tight, trapping some 15,000 people in unheated cars. The 1,100-member New York Stock Exchange shut down. Stranded pedestrians sought refuge in hotels, restaurants, and jails. Sixty-mile-per-hour winds damaged, grounded, or sank upwards of 200 vessels along the coast. In the Tuesday *New York Times,* one reporter described some snow banks as "gigantic Arctic graves." New Yorkers accounted for 200 of 400 fatalities.

Blizzards of such magnitude do not often visit U.S. shores, but when they do, they can strand even weather-wise natives. In Buffalo, New York, a surprise blizzard in January 1977 trapped 17,000 people in offices and on highways, totally paralyzing the city for a week beneath four feet of snow and 30-foot drifts. The blizzard killed 29 people, nine of whom froze in their cars.

In stark contrast, residents of the nation's Rocky Mountain states consider a 21-inch snowfall a mere dusting. On occasion, storms blowing fast and high over the Pacific Ocean will swoop down and clog mountain passes, culminating in horrific avalanches. With frigid northern air pouring into canyons, funneled winds can whip up to 100-mile-per-hour gusts, which can wreck and yank roofs off mountain homes.

In Alaska, storms coming in from the Bering Sea create blinding blizzards with wind chills below -90 degrees Fahrenheit, a temperature that can freeze exposed flesh in seconds. From such Arctic storms glaciers are made. In Antarctica, where average temperatures fall below -58 degrees Fahrenheit, tiny water particles freeze and fall even before they link up into snowflakes. Such diamond dust makes for

beautiful evenings at Earth's frozen poles, because it gloriously scatters moonbeams.

Since Arctic storms seldom strike moderate latitudes, the U.S. East Coast found itself surprised by the Storm of the Century that arrived on March 12, 1993, 105 years to the day after the Blizzard of 1888. Via satellite, forecasters saw the gale coming three days before it hit. Hank Brandli, a veteran meteorologist, called it "the biggest storm I'd ever seen with satellite imagery." Winds of tropical storm strength beat his Melbourne, Florida, home until the blizzard's center hung over northern Maine. Starting in the Pacific Northwest, the storm swooped into the Gulf of Mexico, where—almost like a frozen hurricane—it picked up power and then took off for the north.

Causing 270 fatalities, affecting 26 states, and

Above, a snow plow clears a New York City street during one of several snowstorms in February 1994.

Left, a Chicago building that caught fire during the winter of 1987 is transformed into a mass of ice after firefighters inundated it with water.

Opposite, a mountain of snow all but buries cars and trucks on Interstate Route 95 in Providence, Rhode Island, during a 1978 winter storm.

Farmer Helge Holte of North Dakota was undeterred in tending to his cows during a January 1987 blizzard, above. Windchill during that storm plummeted to -80 degrees Fahrenheit.

Opposite, huge snowdrifts overwhelm an abandoned car along the North Dakota-Canada border during the winter of 1987. Local farmers claim that only a barbed-wire fence stands between frigid arctic blasts and their wheat crops.

leaving $3 billion in property damage, the blizzard broke century-old records. While winds of nearly 130 miles per hour pummeled Mount Washington, New Hampshire, 60 inches of snow piled up in the mountains of North Carolina, where 100 hikers needed rescue. For the first time, all major airports on the East Coast closed for a day. In Florida, as six inches of snow fell in the panhandle, 27 tornadoes trampled 15 counties while a storm surge washed over parts of the state's west coast. Along North Carolina's Outer Banks, 200 surf-pounded houses became uninhabitable, while on New York's Long Island 18 homes fell into the sea. Throughout the southern states, heavy, wet snow collapsed hundreds of roofs and tore down electric lines, leaving 3 million people without power.

New Englanders might have thought themselves finished with such winter nastiness for another century had not January 1994 reminded them of the long-term trend toward winter cold. When the high-altitude jet stream altered its course, exhaling Arctic air onto the northern U.S. plains, a dozen American cities shivered through their coldest days in recorded history. No one can pin down the reason for this apparent cold trend.

Are the big storms since 1989 a blip in the weather charts or a trend to be taken seriously? Should the nation prepare for more monster storms and chills? Forecasters shrug their shoulders and refer back to the Big Picture of climate. All that they can say with confidence is that, despite fears of global warming, North Americans should expect a long-term cold trend over hundreds, perhaps thousands, of years.

"We should realize that what is happening is within the realm of normalcy if you consider climate variation," National Weather Service meteorologist Brad Rippey told the *Wall Street Journal* during the cold spell of 1994. "In other words," the newspaper added, "weather is supposed to be wacky."

From Ice to Fire

Elizabeth Culotta

AROUND A.D. 982, a bold young Viking named Eirik the Red killed some of his neighbors in a quarrel over wooden furniture. Declared an outlaw, and in peril of his life from vengeful enemies in the colony of Iceland, Eirik loaded up his long boat and set sail in the shadow of a glacier. He headed west into the wild, cold seas of the North Atlantic.

After many days at sea he saw land, of a sort: another glacier, this one a mile high, calving giant icebergs into fjords on the eastern shore of a strange island. Undeterred, Eirik traveled southward along the coast until he found an ice-free harbor, where he put to shore. Three years later, his period of exile officially ended, he returned to Iceland bearing tales of a verdant, empty country he called Greenland in hopes of luring his countrymen to live there with him. His stories succeeded, and the next summer several hundred Norse colonists sailed with him on his glacier-marked route to the new land.

For generations, Eirik and his descendants prospered, grazing cattle and sheep despite a short growing season. Eirik named landmarks all over the island after himself, and built a farm with room for 40 head of cattle. In their heyday, the Greenlanders numbered 6,000 in

Page 80: A shimmering 80-foot waterfall descends from an iceberg drifting southward off Canada's Labrador coast. As it enters warmer water, the iceberg will eventually disintegrate.

Pages 82-83: A flow descends from Europe's largest glacier, Hoffellsjök il, in Iceland. As glacial flows converge, streaks of debris merge into a common ridge called a medial moraine, at left.

Pages 84-85: In July 1986, the Hubbard Glacier, one of Alaska's largest ice fields, sends a mass of ice plunging into Disenchantment Bay.

settlements on the western and southern coasts. Around the year 1000, they converted to Christianity; by 1300, they were building grand medieval cathedrals with imported stone and stained glass.

From this stable base, Eirik's sons and daughter ventured even farther west. One son, Leif the Lucky, landed on the shores of North America around 1000. He called this country Vinland because of the "wine berries"—probably cranberries—he saw there. His brother and sister also made trips to the new country and stayed for several years. According to Norse history, early in the eleventh century a boy named Snorri was the first child of European descent born on North American soil.

But what Eirik and his children could not know, as they proudly voyaged the northern oceans, was that they were enjoying a rare period of benevolent weather in Europe, a time historians now call the Medieval Optimum. From about 950 to 1250, Europe enjoyed temperatures a few degrees Fahrenheit warmer than in later centuries. Grapes grew in the hills of Britain, and the French sought to limit imports of English wine.

Then, in the early fourteenth century, the mild weather ceased. All of Europe plunged into a time of erratic climate that ushered in the Little Ice Age. Crops failed and famine erupted from Spain to Russia between 1315 and 1317. In Greenland, the climate turned hostile in one of the most abrupt transformations in the past 7,000 years. The ice thickened, storms battered wildly along the coast, and the already brief growing season became even shorter. Livestock grew thin, and calves died. In the western settlement, desperate colonists ate their dogs to survive. There were no more expeditions to Vinland.

The Norse clung to their farms in the south, but finally even Viking skill could not navigate the ice-choked seas, and the Greenlanders' contact with Europe failed. The last ship on record left for Iceland in 1410. When the next Europeans arrived centuries later, they found only the remains of farms and the shells of the great stone churches.

The Norse perished because they assumed that the climate of the future would be the same as that of the past. When the climate changed, they could not change with it. Yet from the bruising storms of the ice ages to the sizzling droughts and fires of the 1990s, climate is always changing. Millions of years ago, dinosaurs roamed balmy polar forests, while during the most recent Ice Age, much of North America looked like Greenland does today. The more scientists learn, the more volatile climate seems to be. Sometimes conditions evolve gradually, but often the change is violent, with no apparent warning, as in fourteenth-century Greenland. To take an even more extreme example, while Earth was emerging from the last Ice Age, temperatures on Greenland suddenly plummeted 12 degrees Fahrenheit in less than a decade. The world stayed cold for 1,300 years, then leaped back into a warm climate. It seems that rapid, devastating change is simply part of nature's repertoire.

Such flickering between climate settings happens in modern contexts too. Every few years, the Pacific Ocean warms and cools, turning an atmospheric tempest called El Niño on and off. Dryland regions like the Great Plains and the African Sahel may oscillate between decades of rain and drought. All this upheaval takes place on a titanic scale, as giant ocean currents and air masses stream around the globe, leaving a broad trail of flood, drought, and fire in their wake.

Humans are at the mercy of climate, yet we are tampering with what seems to be a crucial climate control: the amount of carbon dioxide in the atmosphere. The burning of fossil fuels is pouring more carbon dioxide into the atmospheric brew, and this particular ingredient may have provoked temperature shifts in ages past. In the 1980s and 1990s, climate seems to have gone awry, with each year bringing a new natural disaster. Is this climatic tumult a first taste of greenhouse warming? The prelude to a new ice age? Or just nature showing who's boss?

In the face of such questions, scientists are moving swiftly to understand the chaotic dance of wind and water, hoping one day to be able to predict climate. They use supercomputers, meteorological measurements, gas bubbles trapped in ancient ice, the dried contents of pack rat middens—any tool they can find to explore climate history and the forces that drive climate. They already have a good understanding of one of the most extreme periods of Earth's

history: The most recent Ice Age, which reached its zenith about 20,000 years ago.

COLD COMFORT

A trip back in time from present-day Chicago to its Ice Age counterpart would reveal the edge of a giant receding ice sheet. Gale-force winds blasted from the height of the glacier to the lakes and rivers below. Giant pieces of ice crashed into the water, while deep blue lakes sparkled on the glacier's surface.

The view in Ice Age Long Island would be much the same. Back then, most of the northern third of North America was buried by glaciers up to one and one-half miles high. Plants, animals, and prehistoric people south of the ice sheets shivered in temperatures as much as 15 to 20 degrees Fahrenheit colder than today's.

Two views of the same mountain and valley—one during glacial flow, the other after the glacier has receded. Opposite, an alpine glacier moves downhill from a bowl-shaped indentation called a cirque, carving out the valley as it progresses. The medial moraine, a ridge of loose debris, cuts down the middle, while a tributary glacier flows in from the right. Above, after the glacier recedes, a forested valley takes shape. The glacier cut truncated grooves along the valley walls, and a mountain lake called a tarn fills the cirque. A hanging valley with a waterfall is left where the tributary glacier encountered the main glacier.

To make a glacier grow, it takes snow as well as cold. So the ice sheets did not move smoothly south from a cap at the North Pole. In fact, parts of the far north, such as Banks Island, which lies within the Arctic Circle in northern Canada, escaped the path of the glaciers. Farther south, the region near Hudson Bay received heavy snowfall, and became a pulsing center of ice development. From this point, great tongues of ice swelled, blanketing landscapes to the south. As the centuries rolled on, the ice finally receded, leaving huge lakes, rivers, and mounds of debris in its wake.

Even during its peak, the formidable glacial landscape covered only part of Ice Age Earth. With much of the ocean's water locked up in glaciers, sea level was about 300 feet lower, and vast tracts of lowland were exposed. Florida was much bigger, and the Carolina coast stretched eastward for many more miles. Just south of the glacier's edge was a narrow band of treeless tundra, where ground squirrels and lemmings scrabbled out a living in boggy ground. Farther south, a rich collection of animals and plants thrived in a giant spruce forest that stretched across much of the central and southern United States. The trees were mixed with grasslike sedge plants, creating an open forest unlike anything on Earth today. Giant beavers flourished in the great glacial rivers, while mammoths and mastodons munched grasses and shrubs. Saber-toothed cats hunted bison and deer, and California condors swooped in to scavenge the carcasses.

People made a good living, too. In Europe 25,000 years ago, Paleolithic hunters chased mammoths and reindeer across the tundra, then retreated to caves to paint images of the animals they revered and hunted. In North America, Paleoindians dined on mastodon, as well as plentiful bison, deer, and elk. But they must have feared the weather. Even beyond the reach of the glacial winds, Ice Age storms are thought to have been more violent than today's.

Human beings have always managed to survive at the edge of glaciers, it seems. In 1991, two German tourists stumbled over the preserved remains of an early glacial traveler in the high Alps bordering Italy and Austria. Called Iceman because he was preserved in a snowdrift near a mountain glacier, this Copper Age explorer lived about 5,000 years ago, long after the continental ice sheets had receded, and conditions were a bit milder than they are now. But he was prepared for clambering over alpine glaciers, wearing a deerskin tunic, leggings and leather boots, and a cape of stout reeds. He carried a copper axe, a short dagger, and a long bow, as well as a primitive medicine kit. His home was perhaps north of the mountains, since his genes show that he was most closely related to modern Germans, Danes, and Icelanders, rather than to southern Europeans or Africans. For unknown reasons, his gear could not protect him on his last journey, and he lay down and died in a rocky hollow, to be preserved for millennia by drifting snow.

The scenery of past ice ages might also be a vision of the future. Today's climate, with the great ice sheets shrunk to harmless caps at the poles, is but a brief interlude between the last deep freeze and the next one. For the past 2.5 million years, Earth has been cycling in and out of glacial states. If the cycles proceed as they have in the past, climate will begin to slide into the next ice age in a few thousand years.

GLACIAL RHYTHMS

For decades, scientists wondered what could possibly cause the Earth to plunge into such a cold climate and back out again. Back in the 1920s, Serbian mathematician Milutin Milankovitch speculated that the waxing and waning of the great ice sheets are related to the

Frozen beneath a Tyrolean glacier for more than 5,000 years, the Iceman emerged in September 1991. Found near the mountainous Austrian-Italian border, his remarkably well-preserved body is one of the oldest ever retrieved intact.

WHITE DAYS, WHITE NIGHTS

Above, a drilling tower protrudes from the dome where scientists retrieve core sections of ancient ice through two miles of Greenland's ice sheet. The researcher at right probes a core sample for clues to climate changes dating back more than 100,000 years.

It was 10 degrees Fahrenheit on a bright and cloudless summer day as the Sun, haloed by a rainbow, slowly circled the horizon. The sparkling snow of the ice sheet stretched for miles in every direction. There were no smells, no insects, and no sounds except the wind. It might have been a typical Ice Age day.

But it wasn't. It was a workday in the twentieth century, and 60 men and women were drilling a core through the center of the Greenland ice sheet to learn how and why ancient climate changed. Four hundred miles north of the Arctic Circle, they lived in an Ice Age climate every summer from 1989 through 1993. "It gives you perspective," says Mark Twickler, associate director of the Greenland Ice Sheet Project 2 (GISP2). "You

realize that if you were in New England 20,000 years ago, you would have been in the same conditions."

Temperatures ranged from a balmy 32 degrees Fahrenheit to -4, and plunged to -40 at the beginning and end of the season. The wind was ever present, whipping flags on tentpoles all night long, and the wind-chill factor was too depressing to calculate. The Sun shone 24 hours a day, since this was polar summer, and on a clear day the view was always the same: white ice fading into blue sky. "It's like being on the ocean, only frozen—you see the horizon all around you," says Twickler.

The scientists' goal: to drill a five-inch core through two miles of ice, pull up the giant icicle in sections, and analyze it for variations in dust, minerals, gases, and other chemical traces that retain clues to past climate.

Some scientists had to work outdoors, but even those who worked inside couldn't stay warm: they had to keep that slab of ice cold. The core processing lab, located beneath

an igloo-like dome, was kept at a toasty 5 degrees Fahrenheit or less. Scientists often donned orange jumpsuits for warmth but had to wear special lightweight gloves to keep the ice core from being contaminated. "Your hands did get cold," admitted Twickler. "There just wasn't much you could do about it." Even so, the Greenland camp was considered soft by glaciologists' standards because it offered hot showers.

Hundreds of miles from civilization, the U.S. team communicated with the outside world by radio and telex, sometimes snowmobiling over to a European ice core drilling site, the Greenland Icecore Project, 18 miles away. There were no trees and no animals except for an occasional sea gull or finch blown far off course in a blizzard. A lone arctic fox appeared one season, but it may have hitchhiked in with the scientists themselves.

"It's cold and flat and white," says Twickler, who lived without a real summer for six years while working on the ice. "But it has romance." ■

way Earth wobbles in space. When Earth's orientation to the sun shifts, the distribution of sunlight on the globe changes, and one hemisphere may warm more than another. Seasons may become more intense or milder, and this can trigger adjustments in the global thermostat. Cool summers, for example, may keep snowpacks high. Once the temperature begins to drop, sparkling white glaciers create their own weather, reflecting sunlight back to space and chilling Earth further.

After making precise calculations of astronomical factors, Milankovitch predicted that cold and warm periods would follow three cycles of 100,000, 41,000, and 23,000 years each. (These cycles are respectively caused by changes in the shape of Earth's orbit, the tilt of Earth with respect to its axis, and the wobbling of the axis over time.)

Milankovitch couldn't prove his theory, because no one could fix a date for the growth and decay of glaciers thousands of years ago. But since the 1970s, scientists have pried such information out of the chemical clues left in ocean sediments, showing that glaciers do indeed grow and shrink in rhythm with the Milankovitch cycles.

Even within a glacial period, climate turns out to be shockingly fickle, lurching between nearly glacial and nearly interglacial conditions at the flick of a switch. Until recent data emerged from twin ice cores drilled at the summit of the Greenland ice cap, no one ever thought that climate could change so fast.

SECRETS OF THE CORES

The ice cores offer a unique window into the past, because they preserve annual snowfall layers from more than 100,000 years ago until now. Scientists can track climate year by year, measuring snowfall, gauging storminess from wind-blown dust, and estimating temperature from the proportion of different oxygen isotopes.

Left, workers at Novyy Urengoy, Siberia, extract 14 trillion cubic feet of gas a year in spite of the weather.

Two roughnecks arrive by helicopter, above, at Nizhnevartovsk, south of Siberia's Samotlor oil deposits. Despite treacherous conditions, the field produces 780 million barrels a year, the world's highest yield.

Left, a woman of the Nentsy people chops wood on the Yamal Peninsula in western Siberia. Nomadic reindeer herders, the Nentsy have thrived near the Arctic Circle for centuries. Now oil and gas development threaten them.

Opposite, Novyy Urengoy's apartment buildings sit atop permanently frozen arctic ground, called permafrost. It is the site of the world's largest natural gas deposit.

A 1983 cyclone blasts Polynesia's Tuamotu Archipelago, sending Arutua atoll residents fleeing for safety. This storm was but one example of the effects of El Niño, a dramatic swing in the global weather cycle that can cause flood, fire, and drought on five continents.

The results are startling. To take just one example, about 11,000 years ago Earth had nearly shaken off its glacial mantle when suddenly, in 10 years or less, temperatures plunged more than 12 degrees Fahrenheit. Near-glacial conditions returned for more than 1,000 years. Polar flowers bloomed again in Europe. Glaciers around the world—in New Zealand as well as Europe—marched forward. Then, even more abruptly, climate leaped into warm, interglacial conditions. In Greenland, the amount of snowfall—symptom of a warmer, wetter climate—doubled in just three years.

That cold spell, called the Younger Dryas, was the last in a long series that shook climate through-

out glacial times. The Little Ice Age of a few centuries ago, when the Potomac River froze and Londoners skated on the Thames River, may have been a milder version of one of these climatic shivers.

The climate's impetuous behavior is unsettling, because it suggests that the system has an on-off switch that can be thrown in as few as 10 years. Even more worrisome is the possibility that such abrupt shifts may have occurred during the last interglacial period, when conditions were similar to those of today but slightly warmer. So far, the ice cores remain ambiguous on this point. But it's possible that the relatively constant conditions of the past 10,000 years, the period in which human civilization developed, mark a freak period of stability in a violently shifting climate.

If the climatic zigzags were triggered by a peculiarity of glacial climate, then our milder age might be immune to such drastic change. But no one knows for sure what caused the rapid fluctuations of the Ice Age. One possible culprit is a slight flickering of the Sun. If the Sun dimmed slightly, the amount of energy striking the upper atmosphere would change, redirecting winds and ocean currents and transforming climate. Sunspots, fiery, gaseous eruptions from the solar surface that signal a brightly burning Sun, may offer a clue. From 1645 to 1715, during the frosty heart of the Little Ice Age, the normal sunspot cycle ceased.

A waning glacial climate might have other switches that could turn the system from warm to cold and back again. For example, there's evidence that thousands of years ago, huge iceberg armadas suddenly calved off the edge of the North American ice sheet and sailed across the Atlantic until they brushed the coast of Europe. These flotillas, symptoms of collapsing ice, set out just before the cold spells ended.

Yet another option is that a massive influx of freshwater, triggered by melting icebergs or glaciers, disrupted the circulation of the briny North Atlantic. A system of currents now ferries heat from the tropics to the northern latitudes. The Gulf Stream is one limb of this conveyor belt of heat, speeding warm surface water up the coast of North America and across to Europe. If that circulation were shut off, as seems to have happened in the past, the North Atlantic would turn bitterly cold. Yet such events in the Northern Hemisphere cannot explain why glaciers also advanced in New Zealand during at least one of the cold spells. Still, the oceans are major players in the climate of any age, including our own. Weather is essentially the ceaseless attempt by wind and water to equalize the temperature from

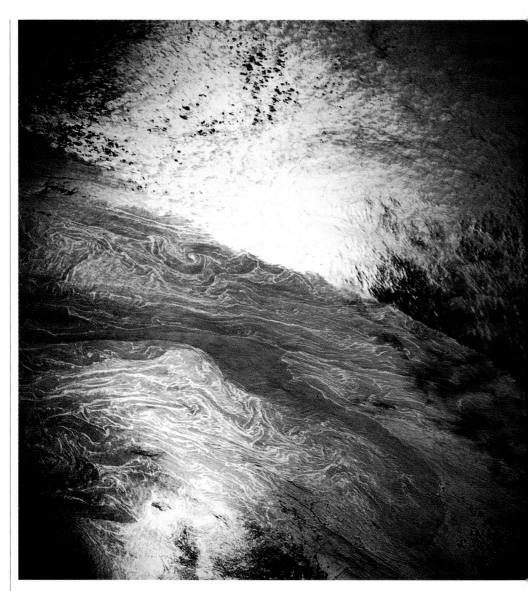

The crew of the space shuttle *Endeavour* took this photograph of the Atlantic Ocean during their September 1992 mission. Their vantage point afforded the crew an excellent view of the sunlight pattern as it moved across the surface of the ocean, highlighting the sharp boundary between the warm, rapidly flowing waters of the Gulf Stream (lower portion) and the cooler, coastal-shelf waters (upper portion).

tropics to poles. Currents and winds chase each other around the globe, carrying heat to the poles and chill to the tropics. The Atlantic currents, for example, gently warm the British Isles and the rest of Europe. Meanwhile, the Pacific Ocean takes center stage in one of the most dangerous recurring climate disasters of the modern world: El Niño.

TIDES AND TEMPESTS

Throughout the winter and spring of 1982, the country of Ecuador was awash. Besieged by torrential rains and flooding, the earth slipped away in deadly mudslides, killing more than

Two million years ago, in what is today's eastern Washington State, a bursting glacial lake churned gravel into ripples 16 feet high and more than 300 feet apart. This great flood did its work south of today's city of Spokane, creating the famed Channeled Scablands.

100 people. Crops and houses were inundated and fisheries failed. All told, the nation lost $400 million to one of the wettest seasons on record.

Half a world away, the bush of southern Australia baked in an unrelenting drought that winter. On February 8, 1983, darkness fell in the middle of the afternoon in Melbourne as a huge dust cloud dumped half a million tons of topsoil on the city. A week later, fierce winds swept fire throughout Melbourne's suburbs and woodlands, killing 75 people and leaving 8,000 homeless.

Meanwhile, in the United States, the Mississippi overflowed its banks and Californians lost 10,000 homes to brutal winter storms. On the islands of French Polynesia, including Tahiti, 25,000 people were displaced by six cyclones in five months.

In Botswana, in southern Africa, drought tightened its grip, stripping fields bare and leaving half the population to subsist on food shipments from abroad. In India, the monsoons failed and crops withered.

From the end of 1982 through the first six months of 1983, the world was besieged by climatic disasters with estimated damages exceeding $13 billion. It was as though a giant hand had pushed the rains thousands of miles off course, so that the moisture desperately needed in Australia and Africa fell with punishing force over North and South America instead.

This immense rearrangement of wind and rain was the fault of El Niño, a capricious climate event that comes every three to six years or so and leaves behind a trail of flood, drought, storm, and catastrophe. El Niño is a teleconnection—a long-distance link among many continents. There's little chance of taming the colossal forces that cause such events, but scientists hope to lessen El Niño's bite by predicting when it will strike.

The phenomenon begins off the coast of South America, where Peruvian fishermen christened it El Niño, the Child, because it arrives at Christmastime. Under normal conditions, trade winds push the warm surface water of the Pacific westward, away from the South American coast. To replace the flow, cold water wells up from below, creating fertile conditions for tiny plants and animals and supporting one of the largest fisheries in the world. Every year in December, this pattern breaks down. The trade winds slacken, the westward current falters. There is little upwelling, bad fishing, and the water temperature warms several degrees. Brief rains shower the coastal Peruvian desert. In a normal year, the trade winds pick up after a few weeks, and the ocean currents return to normal.

Several times every decade, however, El Niño comes early, stays late, and disrupts climate worldwide. The event that drenched Ecuador and ignited Melbourne was the worst on record, but the Child has arrived for the past five millennia at least. It caused the bitter winter of 1976-1977 in the United States, and it returned to spawn more drought and flooding in 1987. In 1991, El Niño came and lingered unexpectedly, contributing to the Midwest floods two years later.

It's not only El Niño that can wreak havoc: La Niña, the opposite pattern, in which abnormally cold temperatures beset the Eastern Pacific, can make trouble, too. In 1988, a La Niña pattern created a sturdy high-pressure system in the eastern Pacific that was implicated in the Midwest drought and Bengal floods that year.

What causes El Niño? The Child seems to be part of a natural, if erratic, oscillation. Its devastations over the past several centuries are recorded in tree rings in the U.S. Southwest and flood markers on the Nile. The ultimate cause may turn out to be periods of high or low solar activity, perhaps related to sunspots, but scientists have not yet proven such a link. However, climatologists have identified the tropical Pacific Ocean as part of the engine behind El Niño and much of the world's climate. Changes there, driven by Earth's rotation and other, unknown factors, start the El Niño cycle.

First, a high-pressure system off the coast of South America weakens. This lessens the trade winds and warps the path of the jet stream, the high-altitude winds that determine the path of storms. As the trades slacken, the pool of warm surface water in the southwestern Pacific expands and pushes eastward. During the 1982-1983 event, that balmy pool stretched for thousands of miles and was more than 12 degrees Fahrenheit above normal.

Understanding all this helps scientists predict El Niño by monitoring the volume of warm surface water in the Pacific. Prediction continues to improve as scientists plug atmospheric and oceanic data into their computer models of climate. On two occasions since 1986, climatologists have been able to herald the arrival of the Child, but so far they haven't been able to predict how severe an El Niño will be or how long it

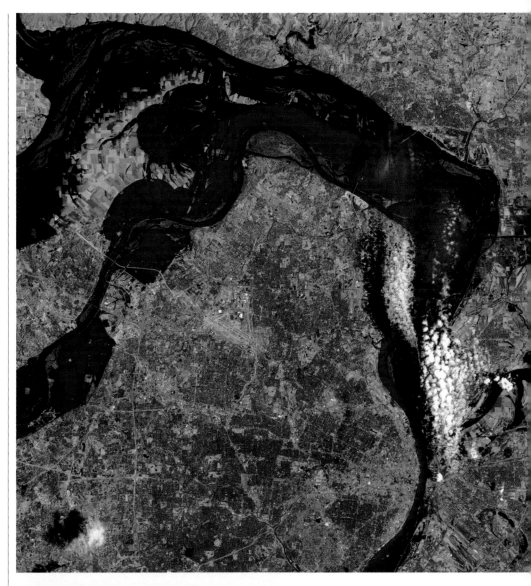

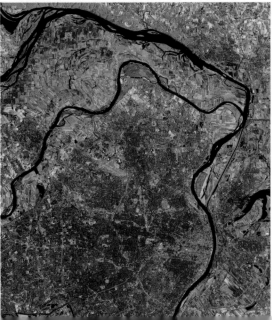

Record rainfall in the central United States during the summer of 1993 brought about the dramatic difference in these two satellite photographs of St. Louis, Missouri: at left, an image taken on July 4, 1988 and above, the same area on July 18, 1993. The land between the Missouri and Mississippi Rivers disappears under the flood waters.

will last. And El Niño is still offering nasty surprises: in 1991, it came and stayed for years,
as though the system was somehow stuck in
the "on" position. In 1993, it was still exerting
its drenching effect on the midsection of
North America.

HIGH SEAS

The flooding caused by an El Niño, devastating
though it may be, is nothing compared to the
massive floods that engulfed Earth's surface in
the past. For thousands of years, floods have
put human life, crops, and property at risk, and
floods occupy a special place in the myths of
cultures around the world. The ancient Greek
philosopher Plato tells of Atlantis, the opulent
civilization drowned "in a single dreadful day
and night." The Australian aborigines have
passed on an oral history detailing the geography
of a land now many feet below the sea. The
Biblical story of Noah echoes a Sumerian and
Assyrian myth, the Epic of Gilgamesh, in which
the gods sent a flood to quench unruly humankind, and only one man and his household survived. In the Assyrian version, the survivor is
called Utnapishtim. Like Noah, he built a giant
ship, loaded it with animals and plants, and rode
it through the days of flooding. When the roaring wind and rain finally ended, Utnapishtim
opened a hatch in his boat and gazed at a perfectly still, flat world, with no sign of life or land.
After the waters ebbed, the gods made him
immortal, and he was said to dwell in the land
from which all the rivers of the world arose.

There's little direct evidence to prove such
legends, of course. But it's true that lands that
once may have been inhabited by people are
now under the sea. The Arafura Sea between
New Zealand and Australia was above sea level
20,000 years ago, as were parts of the Persian
Gulf near the Sumerian empire. And geologists
are convinced that in times past there were

Ama Dablam, in Nepal, above, and the
rest of the Himalayas (which rise to an
altitude of over five miles) enhance the
temperature contrast between land and
sea, strengthening monsoon rains. The
"Roof of the World" alters the path of
the west-east jet stream, affecting the climate throughout the Northern
Hemisphere.

Opposite, dark clouds over Ho Chi Minh
City, Vietnam, in June usually mean torrential rain and flooding. Monsoons are
seasonal shifts in the prevailing winds.
They water the crops of half the world's
people, and act as a massive heat-trans-
fer system.

floods such as the modern world has never known, torrents so powerful that they are called "superfloods" in the scientific literature. These colossal deluges were caused by melting glaciers from 18,000 to 8,000 years ago, during which time the sea level rose about 300 feet. As the ice receded, much of the meltwater pooled in giant lakes, imprisoned by massive ice dams. When the dams broke, the lakes drained catastrophically.

The scars of such a flood are still visible in an area called the Channeled Scablands in eastern Washington State. There, the waters of what was once glacial Lake Missoula were released about 15,000 years ago. The floodwaters scoured basins up to 8 miles wide and 200 feet deep. They cascaded in huge falls, twice the height of Niagara Falls, over what are now dry cliffs. Water washed the lake bed in giant waves, leaving ripple marks 15 feet high. "There's nothing remotely like that flood in modern experience," says geologist Richard Waitt Jr., of the U.S. Geological Survey. "It was equal to the discharge of all the modern rivers in the world together."

But even the Scablands deluge may have been dwarfed by an event about 8,000 years ago. At that time, two vast, connected glacial lakes, Lake Agassiz and Lake Ojibway, lay at the southern edge of the receding Laurentide glacier, filling the Great Lakes basin as well as much of central Canada. When an ice dam at the eastern end of the lakes burst, the water drained violently into Hudson Bay, geologists believe. Such an outpouring of water could have triggered a virtually instantaneous rise in sea level—8 to 16 inches within two days, according to one estimate. The draining of Lake Agassiz was perhaps the largest superflood on the planet, according to some geologists.

Raising sea level by a foot or so doesn't sound like much, but a one-foot rise along the eastern coast of the United States would cause beaches to recede hundreds of feet. In Florida, such a

When moisture-laden air from the Bay of Bengal reaches the Himalayas, storm clouds form and bring heavy rains to India. In the city of Varanasi, above, it is the River Ganges that overflows its banks. In Delhi, left, the floods come from the Yamuna River.

Opposite, cyclone-ravaged Bangladesh is seen in 1991 after an April storm killed 120,000 people. This small agricultural country occupies the delta lands of three major rivers: Ganges, Brahmaputra, and Meghna. Here, cyclones and tidal waves sometimes accompany monsoon flooding.

BLACK SUNDAY

Four Corners, Oklahoma, is swallowed by a dust storm in this 1930 photograph held by a farmer.

Below center, two Kansans venture out during a return of dust conditions to the southern Great Plains in the early 1950s.

On Sunday afternoon, April 14, 1935, seven-year-old Jerry Shannon was standing outside the railroad building in the small town of Felt, Oklahoma, when he looked up and saw the sky darken. "You could see it a-comin," he recalled 34 years later for a reporter from *Smithsonian* magazine. "From the north, here it came, just a whole boil, roll and boil." As the huge black cloud surged toward him, Shannon heard a neighbor praying nearby. "She thought the end of time had arose," he remembers.

Sooty black at its base, dark brown and mauve at the top, the massive storm stretched from west to east as far as the eye could see. This was not the first and certainly not the last of the black blizzards to ravage the Great Plains, but it was destined to become the most infamous.

The roller began by sweeping up dry, powdery topsoil in Wyoming and Colorado. It churned its way southward through Kansas, Oklahoma, and Texas, driving crowds of frightened geese and ducks before it. At 2:40 P.M., it whipped into Dodge City, Kansas, with winds estimated to be 60 miles per hour, and enveloped the town in total darkness for 40 minutes, stranding drivers and short-

ing out car ignitions. Outside of Boise City, Oklahoma, a funeral procession halted in confusion as darkness descended. When the storm roared through Liberal, Kansas, 11-year-old Lila Lee King took refuge at a neighbor's house. She lit matches with trembling fingers but could see almost nothing in the blackness. She thought she was going to die. In Pampa, Texas, Woody Guthrie felt the same way and, as the huge duster approached, he began writing the song "So Long, It's Been Good to Know You."

It was in Guymon, Oklahoma, that the storm made what was perhaps its greatest impact on history. There, an Associated Press reporter named Robert E. Geiger was awed by the gale and the bleak years of drought it represented. The next day, his story in the *Washington (D.C.) Evening Star* for the first time used the words that came to symbolize a decade of drought and depression. Geiger christened the southern Great Plains the "dust bowl of the nation." ∎

rise might swallow as much as 1,000 feet of shore. One-third of the world's people live within 40 miles of a coastline; in the United States, half the population lives within 50 miles of shore. So a significant rise in sea level could devastate such low-lying cities as New Orleans and even threaten entire nations. For example, the Republic of Maldives consists of more than 1,000 idyllic coral islands, with white beaches only a few feet above sea level. A substantial rise in sea level could swamp the country, and even a small increase makes the islanders more vulnerable to the cyclones and storms that batter their shores.

Throughout the past 4,000 years, the period of recorded history, sea level has remained stable. That's why some scientists are concerned about the possibility of higher seas if Earth warms. Worldwide, the sea has risen about six inches in the past hundred years, according to an intergovernmental panel of scientists. It's still rising slowly, at less than a tenth of an inch per year. In cities such as Bangkok and Shanghai, the effective rise is even higher, because human activities—such as siphoning up groundwater for drinking and irrigation—cause the land to sink. As groundwater is depleted, New Orleans, Louisiana, sinks about 1.5 inches per year and Shanghai, China, nearly four inches per year.

If global warming somehow caused the icecaps at the poles to melt completely, the world's oceans would swell by perhaps 250 feet. The U.S. Gulf Coast, for example, as well as much of Florida, Georgia, and the Carolinas, would vanish beneath the sea. But no one expects such a drastic turn of events. Even if climate warms, it's not certain that the icecaps would melt; besides, they wouldn't collapse completely, scientists say. Changing precipitation patterns might create heavier snowfalls at the poles, so the icecaps might actually grow, not shrink.

Still, a rising sea level is likely to be a problem in a warmer world. Although the icecaps may not melt, warmer water expands, so the oceans will probably swell. The Intergovernmental Panel on Climate Change has concluded that if Earth warms as predicted, by about 2.7 to 8.0 degrees Fahrenheit in the next century, sea level may rise at a rate of up to 0.25 inch per year, or by two feet in 100 years. Even if emissions of greenhouse gases are stabilized, sea level would continue to rise for decades or even centuries, as the atmosphere and oceans slowly responded to changing conditions.

Global warming may threaten to inundate parts of the world, but in other regions it raises the specter of drought. Even in a stable climate, rainfall skips capriciously around the globe. A warmer world, while bringing more rainfall and flooding to some areas, may leave others to suffer from long-term drought and the dust and fire that accompany it.

DESERT STORMS

In the United States, the droughts of the 1930s fueled the Great Depression and spurred the migration of tens of thousands of people. But drought can strike anywhere, anytime. It exacts a terrible toll on city dwellers as well as farmers, industrialized societies as well as developing nations. In African nations on the edge of hunger, drought can spawn the tragedy of famine. Even in wealthy California, drought and its sometime companion, fire, can lay waste to cities, as well as to forest and farmland.

What is a drought? The word has more than 150 different meanings, assigned by meteorologists, farmers, economists, hydrologists, and others. It's not simply scarce rainfall, since the amount of moisture that yields a bumper crop in North Dakota might be a drought in Great Britain. Many geographers use a simpler rule of thumb: A drought occurs when there's much less

Above, dust clouds blowing from the Sahel threaten tiny Youdiou, a village of the Dogon people in West Africa's Mali, a nation often challenged by drought.

Right, far away in Rajasthan, India, Hindus wait breathlessly for monsoon rains, the climax of an annual climatic cycle that spells the difference between life and death. From West Africa to Arabia, and across India and Asia into Mongolia and China, a wide swath of hyperaridity shapes cultures and economies.

moisture than people expect and need. For example, in the 1930s, farmers in the southern Plains had high expectations, thanks to bountiful rains in the 1920s. They found out, too late, that those years had been unusually wet.

Throughout the boom decade of the 1920s, railroads and new farming practices were opening up the Plains. Armed with new plows and high hopes, people came in droves to what was then green prairie in Oklahoma, Texas, Kansas, Colorado, and New Mexico. In that time, Oklahoma farmers could buy land for $15 an acre, plow it, sow wheat, harvest 20 bushels per acre, and pay off their land in one season. "Suitcase farmers" came from miles around to plant, plow, and collect their crop and a hefty second income. Professional farmers bought more land and the machinery to work it. They adopted a one-way disk plow that pulverized the soil into a smooth dust, and they used tractors to work ever larger tracts of land. In 1915, there were 3,000 tractors in the state of Kansas; by the start of the Depression there were nearly 70,000. In the southern Plains, the number of acres planted in wheat doubled from 1925 to 1931.

There were whispers, even then, that the weather might not hold. In 1819 explorers had declared the southern Plains part of the Great American Desert. Back in 1860, western dust storms sent black snow to Oberlin, Ohio, and black rain to Syracuse, New York. As late as 1900, the U.S. Geological Survey listed much of the Great Plains as nonagricultural because of scarce rainfall. But with green fields in front of them in the 1920s, few farmers paid attention. The new "scientific" agricultural ideas promoted dust mulch, a layer of fine soil on the surface, to conserve moisture. Agricultural advisers suggested that "rain follows the plow." This wishful thinking seemed to work for a while: the rains came on time, and the harvests were bountiful—60 bushels of wheat per acre in 1926.

Then, starting in 1931, the rains stopped. In 1930, a good year, more than 20 inches of rain fell on Boise City, Oklahoma. Two years later, there were only 12 inches. From 1934 through 1936, the total was only half the normal rainfall—a scant eight or nine inches each year. Exposed from years of unwise farming practices, and with no moisture to hold it, the fine soil blew away.

By 1935, many farmers were just holding on. They grew accustomed to the fine dust, which silently seeped into everything. There was dust in the bathtub, dust on the dishes, dust on the houseplants, dust on the pillow in the morning. Attics collapsed from the weight of tons of topsoil. Farmers died of dust pneumonia. Clouds of grasshoppers and hordes of rabbits overran whatever parched vegetation was left. By 1939, half the state of Oklahoma was on government relief. Thousands of families left, heading for what they hoped were better times in California. Newspaper editor John L. McCarty organized a "Last Man's Club" for anyone who vowed to stay in the Dust Bowl. Caroline Henderson, a panhandle farmer whose letters and essays were published in the *Atlantic Monthly*, spoke for the drought-stricken everywhere: "Impossible it seems not to grieve that the work of our hands should prove so perishable."

UNDER A CRUEL SUN

The Dust Bowl was created by the entwined problems of drought and land degradation, problems that today burden much of the continent of Africa. The same haunting images appear again and again in magazines and newspapers: dying children with their starving mothers, a parched landscape that supports almost no life at all. The misery of famine has returned again and again during the past 25 years to the Horn of Africa and to the Sahel, the belt of semiarid land just south of the Sahara Desert. There,

Above, a Tuareg nomad of Mali wears goggles to protect eyes from blowing sand grains and solar rays.

Pages 104-105: The parched desert landscape of Mali, in Africa's northwest. Scientists see a connection between the weather cycles of Africa and North America. During the 1980s, when Africa's Sahel region suffered a serious drought, the eastern United States enjoyed a vacation from disastrous hurricanes. But by 1989, rains had returned to the Sahel and terrible tropical storms were again hitting the United States. A temperature flip-flop in the tropical oceans may have stimulated the growth of "hurricane seeds," weather cells that sprout near the Sahel and grow as winds steer them toward the Americas.

the grassland steppe has withered and vanished, and soils have deteriorated. In some areas, it seems that the Sahara is marching southward, threatening to engulf the Sahel in waves of sand. But is humankind or nature to blame?

There's no doubt that in parts of the Sahel, "the land is tired," as the Africans say. Decades of overuse, particularly overgrazing, probably play some role. But in the past few years, meteorologists have been reassessing the roles of drought and human impacts on the Sahel—and they are shifting the burden of blame back to the forces of nature.

Even in the best of times, the Sahel could never be called wet. Rainfall is always spotty, on the timescales of both seasons and years. In winter, hot, rainless winds from the Sahara sweep in from the north. If rain comes at all, it comes in the summer, when the wind shifts to the south, bearing moisture-laden air from the Atlantic Ocean.

In the mid-1970s, scientists proposed that human degradation of the land sparked a vicious cycle of drought and desertification. When drought begins, the theory goes, people use the land more intensely, cutting down vegetation and allowing their livestock to overgraze. The stripped soil radiates more heat back out to space, altering local wind patterns and preventing the formation of clouds. In other words, denuding the land keeps the rain away.

But during the late 1980s and 1990s, scientists have begun to question this theory. Although parched landscapes may perpetuate drought by modifying local weather, scientists now emphasize the part played by nature, rather than humans. Meteorologists now recognize that the drought in the Sahel has reached epic proportions in the last 30 years. This region shows the most dramatic decline in rainfall ever recorded by meteorological instruments. From 1961 through 1990, annual rainfall was 20 percent to

40 percent less than from 1931 through 1960. In 1984 and 1990, the Sahel got less than half the normal rainfall of the 1930s through 1950s.

Despite the lack of rainfall, it now appears that the Sahara is not steadily advancing southward as scientists once proposed. From space, parched ground shows up clearly and satellite photos can track the thickness of vegetation at the boundary of the Sahara and the Sahel. From 1980 to 1989, the border undulated back and forth—moving in perfect time with rainfall fluctuations.

Indeed, the Sahel has a long history of dramatic climate change. During glacial times, the Sahel was very dry, but 6,000 years ago, the Sahara and Sahel were both much wetter than they are today. Neolithic fishing villages sprang up beside lakes, and water-loving hippopotamuses were common. These changes are due to differences in Earth's orientation to the Sun, the same subtle shifts that control the waxing and waning of the ice ages. On more familiar timescales, although the dryness of the Sahel is

Mauritanian villagers, above, dig out of a sand dune that drifted into town during a seasonal dry wind. Gales may blow steadily for more than a month.

Opposite, the mud walls of Gao, Mali, in Africa's Sahel, where dust drifts deep as rainless winds blow. Drought cycles, during which the nearby Sahara Desert seems to expand and shrink, have been common to this land for many centuries.

unprecedented in the instrumental record, wild swings in rainfall may be characteristic of the region. Decade-long droughts appear throughout the history of the Sahel, according to lake levels and historical descriptions.

Why does the Sahel's rainfall vary so much? Some have speculated that recent droughts in Africa could be a first sign of human-caused greenhouse warming, but so far there is little evidence for that. Still, scientists are beginning to realize that rainfall in the Sahel is one piece of a giant global puzzle. Just as El Niño in the Pacific Ocean triggers droughts and floods thousands of miles away, the Sahel also appears to be part of a teleconnection. Sahelian rainfall is influenced by sea-surface temperatures far away in the Atlantic Ocean and is correlated with hurricane strength on the U.S. East Coast.

Scientists are still trying to understand the implications of these links. But most are confident of one thing: after the rains return, one day drought will, too. Of course, the tragedy of famine may be lessened even if drought does come. The worst famines of the past few years have erupted in nations such as Somalia, where civil war disrupts food distribution as well as farming. In contrast, after years of drought and a terrible famine in 1984-1985, Ethiopia got its civil affairs in order. Building dams and terracing hillsides, farmers made good use of moderate rains that returned in the early 1990s, perhaps softening the blow when drought struck again a few years later.

TRIAL BY FIRE

Half a world away, drought plagues city dwellers as well as farmers. Just ask the residents of Malibu and Berkeley, California, who saw their neighborhoods destroyed in firestorms during the 1990s. Some fires were sparked by human carelessness or even arson, but the real culprit was the longest drought in recorded California

Above, drought parches Somalia while civil strife transforms a natural disaster into an armed struggle for food and power by rival clans.

Opposite, during an Ethiopian drought in the early 1990s, a refugee drinks her fill at a rescue camp. Water is the most precious commodity in this thirsty land.

Top, in Somalia, a land of famine aggravated by anarchy, a woman of Baidoa covers her face with netting to keep swarms of flies from settling on tears and discharge from her infected eyes.

Above, people of the eastern cape, the Horn of Africa, have seen many famines, including man-made ones in which one political or military faction cut supplies to starve out other, weaker groups. To survive, hungry people flee their homes, gathering at places like Koren Camp in Ethiopia in 1984.

Opposite, wasted from famine and thirst, children wait for daily rations at Mekele Camp in Tigray, Ethiopia. Those unable to reach such food distribution sites often perish.

history. Years of dryness browned trees and shrubs, creating a tinderbox ready to blow.

That's what happened on the hot Sunday morning on October 20, 1991, when a dry east wind blew embers from a grassfire into the Oakland-Berkeley hills. Back in 1923, similar conditions in this neighborhood of tree-lined streets set off a conflagration that razed 600 homes in one hour. This time, there was more to lose. The firestorm vaulted quickly from wilderness to suburbia, devouring coyote brush and million-dollar wooden homes with equal greed. Firefighters saw flames soaring 100 feet high and estimated temperatures at 2,000 degrees Fahrenheit. From the air, the blaze looked and acted like a whirling tornado of flame. It leapt from roof to roof, torching homes at the rate of one every 11 seconds. After 10 hours, 25 people were dead and 3,000 homes incinerated. Total damage: $1.5 billion. It was the worst blaze in California history since the catastrophic 1906 fire in downtown San Francisco.

Even the rich and famous found themselves homeless, if only temporarily. Retired baseball star Reggie Jackson, whose Oakland home was destroyed, was quoted as saying, "It strips you. You're helpless. Defenseless."

By the next day, the weather had cooled, the wind had stilled, and in the wee hours of the morning, fog settled in as usual. The firestorm was over, but the drought was not. Even in the best of times, California has no surplus of water. The state's average annual rainfall is 23 inches per year, compared to more than 40 inches in Washington, D.C., and New York City and more than 50 inches in Florida. California rains are concentrated in winter, thanks to a high-pressure system that sits offshore in the Pacific Ocean all summer and diverts storms from the coast. Every October, vegetation is parched and dry after months without rain. From about November to April, the sunlight and high pressure move south,

Above, Mali women do their part to combat desertification on a women's farming co-op in Sokonafing.

Opposite, after 30 years of civil unrest and mismanagement of water resources, Ethiopian residents of the Tigray region return to their land to build an earthen dam as part of a soil and water conservation program.

and storm systems can stream into California.

In the late 1980s and early 1990s, however, those systems didn't come. It was the longest drought in the state's history, from 1987 to late 1992. Deadwood was plentiful, left by dry-weather insects such as the bark beetle and nurtured by years of fire suppression. Small fires burn up stocks of deadwood, but in suburban areas such fires can be dangerous and are extinguished as fast as possible. As a result, when a large fire erupts, there's more wood to burn. Geographers once compared the fire histories of suburban San Diego County, where fires are suppressed, and the undeveloped hills of Baja California, where small brushfires are allowed to burn. The worst infernos raged in San Diego.

California received rain at last in the winter of 1992-1993. But there was still plenty of deadwood available. Fire roared again in late October 1993, when a series of 21 blazes raged through Southern California, devouring estates in Malibu and Laguna Beach. Four people died, and more than 1,000 homes were destroyed, with total losses of more than $1 billion.

A year later, many of the incinerated homes have been rebuilt, though in accordance with stricter fire-prevention codes, and the rains have stayed steady. But firefighters continue to suppress brushfires to protect homeowners. Drought is almost certain to return sometime, and if predictions for future global warming are correct, it may return sooner.

Indeed, the recent drought is child's play compared to the colossal dry spells that parched the state in centuries past. New studies of past climate reveal that during the Middle Ages, while Vikings sailed the northern seas, the Sierra Nevada of California baked in unrelenting drought for decade after decade. Scientists analyzed data from tree rings in stumps now drowned in lakes, marshes, and streams, and found that water levels were very low from

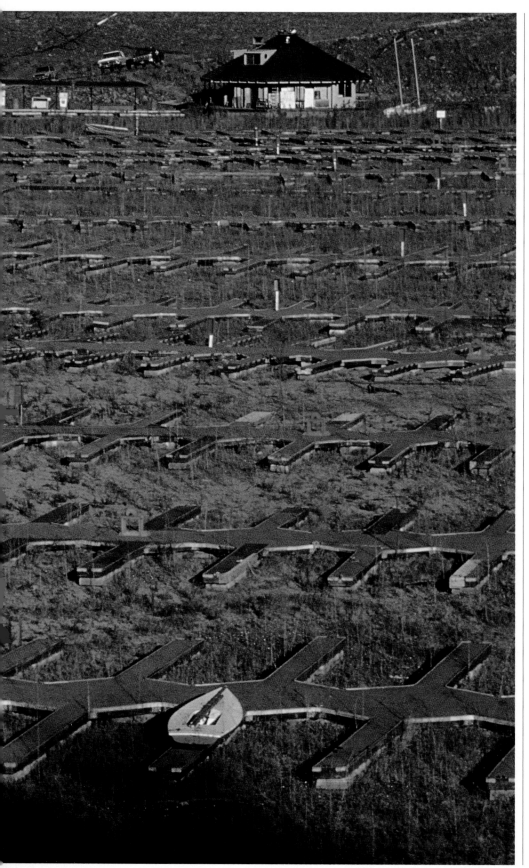

892 to 1112, and again from 1209 to 1350. This period was considered the Medieval Optimum by Europeans, but in the Americas, the extreme climate conditions may have helped topple civilizations such as the Anasazi of the western United States, who vanished in the early fourteenth century. If global warming comes, and if warmer conditions in the future repeat the patterns of the past, then Californians may face devastating droughts in the next century.

BREATH OF A PLANET

In the early Jurassic period in what is now Antarctica, a 25-foot-long crested dinosaur hunted its prey through a cool, humid forest. Plant-eating dinosaurs munched primitive trees and ferns in a climate similar to that of the Pacific Northwest today. When the carnivore died, smaller dinosaurs gathered around the huge carcass to gnaw the bones, while pterosaurs soared overhead.

In the same spot nearly 200 million years later, paleontologist William Hammer of Augustana College braved temperatures of -35 degrees Fahrenheit to retrieve the fossilized bones of those dinosaurs. It was so cold that the ink in his ballpoint pen froze, and he had to write his field notes in pencil. Hammer carved a ton of rock from the barren cliffs of the Transantarctic Mountains and carried the weighty booty back to warmer climes. There, he pieced together evidence of a thriving community of dinosaurs. A glacier had scoured away part of the snout of the big predator, but the flaring crest on the creature's head, some limb bones, and the shearing teeth of a meateater remained. Hammer called the dinosaur *Cryolophosaurus ellioti*, or frozen crested reptile, because he nearly froze to death collecting it.

What caused the metamorphosis of Antarctica from a cool forest into a lifeless icefield? As always with climate, many forces act together.

But many geologists suspect that, over the long history of Earth, carbon dioxide has been a key catalyst of change. Millions of years before humans evolved, Earth was draining carbon dioxide from the atmosphere to the oceans, capturing the carbon in rocks deep underground, and eventually exhaling it into the air through volcanoes. By changing the rhythm of this long, slow respiration, the planet may regulate its temperature, using the thickness of its atmospheric blanket of carbon dioxide to set the global thermostat.

Such climatic effects are possible because carbon dioxide in the atmosphere acts like glass in a greenhouse. In the daytime, it allows sunlight to pass through and shine on the Earth. At night, when the planet reradiates solar energy as heat, carbon dioxide and other greenhouse gases trap that heat and warm the world. This bit of atmospheric physics is of great interest today, as humans pump tons of carbon dioxide into the air each year. But variations in the concentration of carbon dioxide in the atmosphere are more than just a feature of the industrial age—they may have shaped life on Earth.

To explore the long-term connections between carbon dioxide and climate, geologists turned first to the ice cores, which offer an unparalleled window into the climate and atmosphere of the past. Tiny gas bubbles trapped in the glacial ice on Greenland and Antarctica retain the chemistry of ancient air, while dust and other elements offer clues to past climate. From this storehouse of data, scientists have concluded that over the past 150,000 years, the concentration of carbon dioxide in the atmosphere has risen and fallen in relative synchrony with global temperatures. During the last Ice Age, the amount of carbon dioxide in the air was thinned by about 30 percent. It's harder to estimate how much of the gas was present millions of years ago, but the harmony between carbon dioxide and climate seems to extend

Left, a withered corn crop, parched by the drought that struck Georgia in 1986, signals the end of Henry Wood's farming career.

deep into the past, as Earth cycles through a long progression of "icehouses" and "greenhouses." When *Cryolophosaurus* hunted its prey in Antarctica, it probably breathed air richer in carbon dioxide than we do today.

The mechanism of this global temperature control may be the way carbon cycles through air, oceans, and rock, according to a theory developed recently by geologists. In the air, carbon dioxide dissolves into water droplets and rains onto the surface. It erodes rocks and is eventually carried off to sea, where it is deposited onto the seafloor as calcium carbonate. Over time, these sediments are buried, and slowly

North Dakota farmer Lowell Nelson, above, surveys his dusty field, caused by the summer 1988 heat wave that resulted in $40 billion of damage in the central and eastern United States.

Opposite, left high and dry in the California drought that began in 1987, docks and dead fish litter the dry bed of the Sacramento River in July 1990.

Venus, Earth, and Mars, top to bottom, share a similar composition—rocky exteriors over cores that are believed to be metal. Unlike temperate Earth, no known life forms exist on steamy Venus. Its surface temperatures reach 890 degrees Fahrenheit, while frigid Mars ranges from -189 degrees to -9 degrees Fahrenheit. Earth temperatures range between -60 degrees and 130 degrees Fahrenheit.

turn to rock. Ultimately, the cycle of plate tectonics pushes these rocks deep within Earth, where high temperatures and pressures liberate carbon dioxide and return it to the atmosphere via volcanoes.

The beauty of the cycle is that it slowly buffers the effects of other climatic forces. For example, if the Sun were dimmer, as it was 3.5 billion years ago when Earth was young, the climate might cool. That would decrease rainfall, since cooler air evaporates less water from the oceans. Less rainfall means less erosion of rock and more carbon dioxide in the atmosphere, thus insulating Earth. As the Sun grew brighter over hundreds of millions of years, rainfall and erosion would increase, and carbon dioxide would drain from the atmosphere more quickly.

Life influences the cycle and so does plate tectonics. When the giant plates of Earth's crust move rapidly, carbon dioxide is more quickly released from its rocky prison. During the torrid Cretaceous period, 100 million years ago, dinosaurs were wandering near the poles, and volcanoes hissed and boiled throughout the world, mixing an atmospheric brew that contained perhaps several times as much carbon dioxide as today's.

This colossal cycle may explain what geologists call the Goldilocks paradox of the planets: Mars is too cold to support life, Venus is too hot, but Earth is just the right temperature. Of course, Mars is farther from the Sun and Venus is closer, but that's not the whole explanation, according to a theory worked out by scientist James Kasting and others. Mars was once apparently warm enough to have liquid water, but today has almost no atmosphere and a surface climate that resembles winter in Antarctica. Sometime in the past, the planet apparently stopped exhaling carbon dioxide from its interior. Today, most of the carbon remains locked up

in rock rather than in the air, and Mars is a dead planet. Venus represents the other extreme. Nearly all of its carbon dioxide has flowed into the atmosphere, and a runaway greenhouse effect has created an inferno with surface temperatures of up to 890 degrees Fahrenheit.

All this supports the notion that carbon dioxide is indeed a crucial climatic control, a built-in thermostat. If so, humans have been fiddling with the dial since the Industrial Revolution. Every year, carbon dioxide is dug up from its burial place in fossil fuels and released into the atmosphere at a rate of approximately 7 billion tons per year. The expected result is a warmer climate. But the detailed outcome of this global experiment is hard to predict. To help, scientists plug thousands of equations into supercomputers to create a simulated climate. The models are only a rough approximation of real climate, but coupled with data on past climate changes, these supercomputer creations are the best forecasting tools on hand.

Since the Industrial Revolution began, the amount of carbon dioxide in the atmosphere has increased by about 25 percent. Other greenhouse gases are on the upswing, too—methane, for example, has more than doubled. The temperature side of the equation is murkier. Evidence from many sources—including meteorological records, ocean temperatures recorded in ships' logs, boreholes drilled in soil, and the shrinking of mountain glaciers, to mention just a few—points to a global warming of about one degree Fahrenheit in the past 100 years. But that slight warming is within the range of natural climate variability, so scientists don't know if it is due to an enhanced greenhouse effect or not.

Furthermore, the present-day carbon cycle continues to offer surprises. For instance, more than 3 billion tons of carbon—nearly half the amount pumped into the atmosphere each year—are missing, meaning that climatologists don't know where this carbon goes. It's not in the atmosphere, and although it might be absorbed by the deep ocean or the forests, no one knows for sure. Then there are clouds, which can either warm the planet by trapping heat or cool it by reflecting sunlight. The pollutant sulfur dioxide adds yet another complication, because, like carbon dioxide, it is released when fossil fuels are burned. But sulfur dioxide tends to reflect light back into space and have a short-term cooling effect.

Another unforeseen turn of events began in the early 1990s, when the amount of carbon dioxide in the air stopped rising or even dipped a bit. Scientists don't know why, although the timing makes them suspect the 1991 eruption of Mount Pinatubo. Some speculate that minerals from the eruption rained onto the oceans and sparked enormous blooms of plankton that sucked additional carbon dioxide from the air.

Despite such surprises, carbon dioxide is still pouring into the atmosphere, and its concentration in air is expected to keep rising. As for temperature, the long-term forecast has been agreed upon by an international panel of scientists. When the amount of carbon dioxide doubles, probably sometime in the next century, Earth is predicted to warm by about 2.7 to 8.0 degrees Fahrenheit. Such a warming could have profound effects, warns the Intergovernmental Panel on Climate Change. Computer predictions call for more warming in temperate latitudes and less in the tropics. Rain and snow will probably increase in some areas and decrease in others, but such details are quite fuzzy. Likely a catalyst of change in the past, carbon dioxide may continue its role in shaping the climate of the future.

WINDS OF CHANGE

Droughts, floods, blizzards, hurricanes—could it be that global warming has already begun? In the waning years of the twentieth century, some

of the world's most wicked weather erupted in the United States. In 1988, drought parched crops, dried the Mississippi to a trickle, and held up barge traffic for months. Five years later, the barges were berthed once more, this time thanks to a hundred-year flood so ruinous that entire towns packed up and moved to higher ground. In August 1992, the most expensive hurricane ever slammed Florida; six months later, the Northeast was treated to what meteorologists called the Blizzard of the Century—a freak cyclone that killed 26 people in Florida and dumped 40 inches of snow in upstate New York. From 1986 through 1992, Californians struggled

Left, prompted by a statewide, six-year drought that ended in 1993, Los Angeles' strict water conservation laws are enforced by "drought busters" such as Tony Marufo who patrol neighborhoods in search of violators.

Above, a Lindsey, Ohio, resident wets down a withering tree during the drought of 1988.

Pages 118-119: A vast, billowing smoke cloud, produced by the Malibu fires of October 1993, obscures part of the California coastline. Alarmingly, most of the more than 20 major blazes that blackened 200,000 acres of Southern California over a two-week period in the fall of 1993 are thought to have been set by arsonists.

Above, one of the expensive Malibu beachfront properties threatened by the roaring inferno.

Opposite, enshrouded by smoke and flames, a Laguna, California, resident and two firefighters make a heroic stand against the conflagration that consumed 10,800 acres and 361 homes in this area on October 27, 1993.

through drought, and in 1994 the East Coast was blasted by an icy winter that never seemed to end.

The savage weather didn't stop its assaults at the U.S. border. In the 1980s and 1990s, Bangladesh was battered by floods, Australia and Africa sizzled in drought, and in Hong Kong the rains were so bad that meteorologists invented a new term—black rainstorm alert—to describe dark skies and torrential rains ahead. There's an old saying that climate is what you expect, weather is what you get. But a look at the climate disasters of the past century or two—the period for which meteorologists have detailed measurements—may help put recent events in perspective.

The climate dial does seem to have been reset somewhat during the 1980s and early 1990s. Worldwide, the 1980s were the hottest decade on record. In the United States, only the blistering years of the 1930s and the 1950s were warmer than the 1980s. Climatologists agree that the planet has warmed slightly in the past century, by about one degree Fahrenheit. But the changes go beyond temperature. The 1980s also ushered in a period of frightening climatic variability, when disaster after disaster struck populated areas. The insurance industry reeled from major losses, and one study estimated that there were 94 percent more natural disasters in the 1980s than in the 1970s. Precipitation fluctuated wildly. In 1983, nearly half the United States was drenched in what meteorologists called "severely to extremely wet conditions," in the soggiest such spell this century. Drought struck only a few years later in the Midwest and California. In terms of rain and snow, the 1980s were the most variable decade on record, according to the National Climatic Data Center (NCDC) in Asheville, North Carolina. The 1990s continued this roller coaster of rainfall and temperature, and in the East the previous

warming trend ended abruptly in frigid winters.

In a few cases, this upheaval matches computer predictions of the results of a stronger greenhouse effect. For example, the models foretell more warming at higher latitudes, as has happened in the past century. Models also predict that warmer tropical ocean temperatures will spawn stronger hurricanes, a forecast survivors of Hurricane Andrew have no trouble believing.

Despite such points, climatologists aren't ready to ascribe the recent tumult to a stronger greenhouse effect. At any given moment, climate is influenced by a host of interacting factors, each working on its own timescale. It's almost impossible to discern a single, linear chain of cause and effect in this web of shifting relationships. That's why climate is a premier example of chaos: the system is so fiercely complex that the details of its behavior are intrinsically unpredictable.

Still, some signals come through strongly enough for climatologists to read. For example, Easterners who shivered through the winters of the early 1990s can put at least part of the blame onto the eruption of Mount Pinatubo in the Philippines. That cataclysm spewed tons of sulfuric acid particles into the stratosphere, where they reflected sunlight back into space and cooled Earth's surface by a degree or two.

It could have been worse: another well-known volcanic eruption, the explosion of Mount Tambora in the nineteenth century, spawned the Year Without a Summer in 1816. Frost blighted crops in July in New England that year, and, in Europe, torrential rain from May to October spoiled harvests and prompted political unrest.

Mount Pinatubo has certainly altered the climate, but what about all the weird weather that happened before Pinatubo exploded? The blame for some events, such as the worldwide floods and droughts of 1982-1983, can go to El Niño, which altered temperatures and storm tracks throughout the world. But then the question becomes, what caused such a massive El Niño? And why did the 1991 El Niño linger for years instead of shutting off as usual? The answers to those questions are unknown.

When simple cause-and-effect explanations fail, a statistical survey may help. Compared to the 1960s and 1970s, the 1980s and 1990s are full of wild weather. In fact, although the 1960s epitomize social upheaval, in the United States they were among the most stable decades of the century, climatologically speaking. Old-timers who lectured the younger generation on the terrible storms of yesteryear were telling the truth: the climate was worse—or at least more erratic—from the 1930s through the 1950s. With the advent of the 1980s, it seems that the U.S. climate has entered another period of variability.

Take hurricanes. The fury of Hurricane Andrew in 1992 was both terrifying and unexpected, because it was the worst in years. But according to the NCDC, the period from 1965 to 1985 saw a drop in the average maximum wind speed of hurricanes, when compared to the previous 60 years. During the 30-year period of relatively mild tropical storms, few governments spent much time or money on hurricane emergency management plans. Now, sensing that a new era has begun, emergency plans for hurricanes are once again a priority, as they were in the 1940s and 1950s.

Then there's winter. The winters of the 1990s have certainly been bitter on the East Coast, but their impact was no doubt enhanced by the fact that from 1980 to 1992, the nation enjoyed a stretch of unusually mild winters, with relatively little snow. When winter returned at full strength, it was a shock. Statistically at least, the best analog for the present climate may be the 1930s and 1940s. The Dust

Above, in Topanga Canyon, one of hundreds of canyons down which super-heated, incendiary Santa Ana winds rush from the Mojave Desert to the Pacific, a helicopter makes a water drop on an advancing fire line.

Far left, battle-fatigued Los Angeles County firefighters rest on a sidewalk after engaging the November 3, 1993, Malibu fire.

Left, a smile graces the soot-covered face of a weary California Department of Forestry firefighter.

Above, an Oakland, California, resident weeps upon seeing the burned-out shell that was once his car. The vehicle was destroyed by an intensely hot, wind-driven brush fire that swept through Oakland on October 20, 1991.

Opposite, rows of blackened chimney stacks loom over a deep ashen carpet where homes stood before the Oakland inferno.

Bowl years are best known for drought, but the decade began with devastating floods in 1931, and floods and hurricanes recurred in 1936 and 1937. Indeed, the extreme weather of the time spurred government to try to prepare better for climate change, and the present incarnations of the Soil Conservation Service and the Army Corps of Engineers were the result.

So what's normal climate—the seesaw of the 1930s or the tranquility of the 1960s? It depends on the definition of normal. Meteorologists have agreed on an international definition: the statistical average of weather over three consecutive decades. But many areas of the world, such as the Great Plains or the Sahel, naturally fluctuate between climate extremes on the scale of decades. Typical climate for the Sahel in 1995 is quite different from typical climate between 1930 and 1960. So an "abnormal" climate may be atmospheric business as usual.

Even those who expect a warmer world agree that the recent mishmash of climate extremes is within the range of natural variability. "Climate changes all the time, by definition," says Richard Heim of the NCDC. "I can't say that in the United States we're having a massive climate change. There are climate fluctuations, but nothing like what's happened in the past."

No matter what's causing the turbulence, the extreme climates show few signs of abating. El Niño seems likely to continue to flip on and off—or perhaps stay on and confound expectations even more. The oceans continue to creep slowly onto the shore. Mount Pinatubo has subsided, but active volcanoes around the world still bubble. In response, climatologists are working overtime to understand how climate works and how the air and oceans interact with Earth's cycles of mountain building and subduction. For now, forecasters have only one bit of advice for those curious about the future: when it comes to climate, expect the unexpected.

THE UNSTABLE EARTH

RICHARD MONASTERSKY

WHILE MOST of California's San Fernando Valley slumbered, a faint electronic hum roused Shannon Jones out of her dreams. No matter which way she turned, the college student could not escape the fuzzy electronic sound emanating from across the room. She finally dragged herself out of bed at 3 A.M. to turn off the offending television set. Maybe now she could get some much-needed rest before launching into a full day of practice with the nationally ranked Cal State-Northridge softball team. But even as the star third-baseman slipped back into sleep that early January morning, a long dormant fault 12 miles underground started to stir.

In the neighboring apartment building, a lonely light streamed out of a third-floor window belonging to Donald Hall. The English teacher had hours ago surrendered to insomnia and was sitting at his desk catching up on some work. Like many Californians, Hall was a transplant, a native Alabamian who had headed west after graduate school and a stint in the Peace Corps. Although he hadn't grown up in California, Hall would recognize the earthquake before most native Angelenos even knew what had hit them. No doubt the insomnia gave him a head start. But something else helped as well. Back in his childhood, Hall had twice lived through

Right, a serene Los Angeles skyline masks the destruction that has occurred during eight major earthquakes in the past 90 years.

Center, the January 17, 1994, earthquake reduced houses to rubble. About 25,000 dwellings were damaged and more than 20,000 people were left homeless.

Bottom, the 1994 quake derailed freight cars in the San Fernando Valley.

Opposite, water gushes from pipes and gas explodes from a broken main along Balboa Boulevard in Los Angeles.

Page 126: An aerial view of residential dwellings destroyed by a 1971 earthquake that hit the San Fernando Valley. The quake measured magnitude 6.5.

Pages 128-129: A Honda lies crushed under a portion of the Golden State Freeway in Los Angeles on January 17, 1994. That morning, Californians were rattled awake by L.A.'s worst earthquake in 23 years. It measured magnitude 6.7, killed 61, and left close to 6,000 injured.

Pages 130-131: Gas mains fractured by the January 17 earthquake sent plumes of fire shooting into the air. The explosions melted nearby car windows.

the terror of watching tornadoes pass not more than a few hundred yards away. That experience had left him attuned to the sounds of disaster.

A few miles to the west of Hall's apartment complex, Jewell Rhodes smiled at the smell of fresh coffee her husband had just brought into the bedroom. Although it was only 4:15 A.M., Jewell's work beckoned. Her first novel, published a few months earlier, had garnered a string of favorable reviews around the country. Now she was well into a second book. With two children and her classes to teach, she had to squeeze writing in during her spare time, which meant when everyone else slept. Her husband, Brad, flicked on the portable computer and crawled back into bed to cherish a few moments with Jewell before she started her workday.

As the two chatted quietly, the ground beneath their house—beneath Jones, Hall, and all of Northridge, California—reached the breaking point. Mountains to the north and south had slowly squeezed the San Fernando Valley until the crust could no longer stand the strain. At 4:31, the rock finally snapped. A tiny crack raced underground, reaching a mile in length in less than a second. Then it hesitated.

Had the action ended there, this slight readjustment of the valley floor would have remained a minor quake, registering no more than magnitude 4. But it didn't. A tough patch of rock had merely slowed the fracture down. It sliced through this barrier and then shot up through the crust, ultimately rupturing a circular patch six miles across.

Now free after so many years, the blocks that make up the valley floor suddenly shifted position. Mountain ranges on either side lurched higher and closer together, relieving stress that had built up since the days when orange groves covered much of Los Angeles. Such wholesale movement of solid rock sent volleys of seismic energy rocketing toward the surface at 13,500 miles per hour.

The first waves hit Jewell and Brad's floor with explosive force. It sounded as if someone had set off a cannon in their living room while simultaneously smashing the house against a concrete wall. Without a word, without even wondering what had happened, the two sprang out of bed and sprinted toward their children's rooms. They had reached the hallway before the word "earthquake" surfaced in Brad's mind.

Somewhere in the city, a power transformer blew and the house went black. Brad flung himself on top of his six-year-old daughter, hoping to protect her from the window above her bed or the ceiling, should it collapse. In the darkness, Jewell weaved across the dancing floor to her son's room and grabbed the wailing three-year-old. Then the family huddled through the aftershocks, with only the dim glare of the battery-powered computer to light the room.

Donald Hall, at work in his dining room, knew from the outset that the quake would tear his building apart. The apartment complex had swayed excessively two years earlier when a distant tremor had struck the Mojave Desert, more than 100 miles away. This one would be much worse, he thought, judging from the tremendous rumbling that sounded like one of the tornadoes of his childhood.

Hall had already prepared for this moment. Even before objects started falling from the shelves, he raced through the kitchen toward a small hallway. Crouched low to the ground, Hall braced his arms against either wall. Wave after wave of seismic energy jerked the building forward, backward, side to side, even up and down. For 30 seconds, Hall rode out the tremor, hearing all that he owned crash to the floor. The apartment complex itself groaned as part of it gave way, crushing rooms and garages on the first floor.

In the building next door, Shannon Jones was sleeping in one of those first-floor apartments.

Right, this mural was damaged during the 1994 Los Angeles earthquake.

Below, dirt and boulders, shaken loose by the quake's early morning tremors, ripped through the walls of Starr Sutherland's Malibu home, crashing into the living room, kitchen, and bedrooms. Total damage in the L.A. area was estimated at $15 billion.

Right, T-shirts for sale on the streets of Los Angeles after the 1994 earthquake add a touch of humor to an otherwise disastrous situation.

Opposite, a line of cars lies beneath a toppled building.

The softball player instantly woke up with the first jolt, wondering what was happening. It didn't matter, since she had no time to think. With athletic instinct, she raised her forearm above her head just in time to block a falling piece of the ceiling. She ran through the darkness toward the bedroom door that led to an interior hallway. Then she hesitated.

Something made her turn around and race in the opposite direction. Stepping on broken glass, the barefoot student jumped through her shattered bedroom window into the shrubbery outside. Moments later, the ceiling fell, crushing the very hallway toward which Jones had originally headed. The collapse killed 16 of her neighbors on the first floor.

When the shaking stopped, cries from the trapped and the injured broke the silence. "That was the most devastating part of the whole thing—hearing people scream when you couldn't do anything for them," Jones says. "We didn't know where they were, we didn't have any shoes, no flashlights. There was no stairwell left, so we couldn't even get to them."

In all, the Northridge earthquake on January 17, 1994, claimed 61 lives and caused more than $15 billion in damage. Aside from Hurricane Andrew in 1992, the San Fernando Valley jolt rang up the largest disaster bill in U.S. history. But with a magnitude of 6.7, the quake didn't even reach the big league. For instance, it released only one-thirtieth the energy of the Great 1906 earthquake near San Francisco, which had an estimated magnitude of 8.2.

What made the Northridge earthquake so devastating was its proximity to people. Unlike many recent California earthquakes, this one hit directly beneath a metropolitan area, unleashing its full force on the populace above. The disaster's toll teaches the disturbing lesson that even moderate shocks can bring a city to its knees. And Los Angeles got off light this time. Had the

quake struck in the middle of a workday, experts say, the death toll could have reached into the thousands.

The Northridge quake occurred on a hidden, unknown fault, one of several that cut directly beneath the Los Angeles area. This fact unsettles seismologists because it means that many more Northridge-size quakes, and possibly even large shocks, are waiting to break right beneath the city.

RECIPE FOR AN EARTHQUAKE

When the once solid ground shakes and rolls underfoot, tossing people about like rag dolls, the laws of nature seem to collapse into chaos. But earthquakes, volcanic eruptions, and other terrifying manifestations of the unstable Earth are completely natural—and inevitable. They have shaken *Homo sapiens* from the beginning, even from the time that early human ancestors began walking upright on the quake-plagued plains of East Africa.

Throughout history, societies hit by such natural disasters have quelled their fears by seeking explanations in religion. The Maya in Central America blamed earthquakes on four gods charged with supporting the corners of the Earth. Whenever these beings observed humans growing too numerous, they would shake and tilt the ground to trim the population. According to an old Japanese myth, their island chain rested on the back of the *namazu,* a giant catfish that occasionally flapped its body wildly when the attention of the gods slipped.

The Hawaiians believed the volcano Kilauea erupted whenever its resident divinity, Pele, displayed her notoriously short temper by lashing out at siblings or lovers. The Romans worshipped Vulcan, the god of fire, who kept his blacksmith's forge within a mountain off the coast of Italy. From his name comes the word volcano.

Searching for some explanation more satisfy-

This satellite image, above, shows the area covered by the Great Rift, where the Somali and African tectonic plates draw away from each other. Spanning 3,500 miles, it affects a dozen East African nations.

Opposite, East Africa's Great Rift slices south across Kenya, its western wall rising above Little Magadi, one of the region's soda lakes. In this semi-desert, whales may someday graze on plankton; geologists predict the rift will break open and fill with seawater at the Afar Triangle, where the Red Sea meets the Gulf of Aden.

Right, during the 1989 Loma Prieta earthquake, south of San Francisco, the San Andreas Fault ruptured about 11 miles beneath the surface—at the earthquake's hypocenter. White curves show the energy radiating in every direction. When the fault ruptured, the Pacific plate slipped six and one-half feet past the North American plate and also moved upward about three feet.

Below, Charles Richter studies seismic readings in his California office. During the 1930s and 1940s, Richter, along with Beno Gutenberg, developed the best-known system for measuring the intensity of earthquakes—the Richter scale.

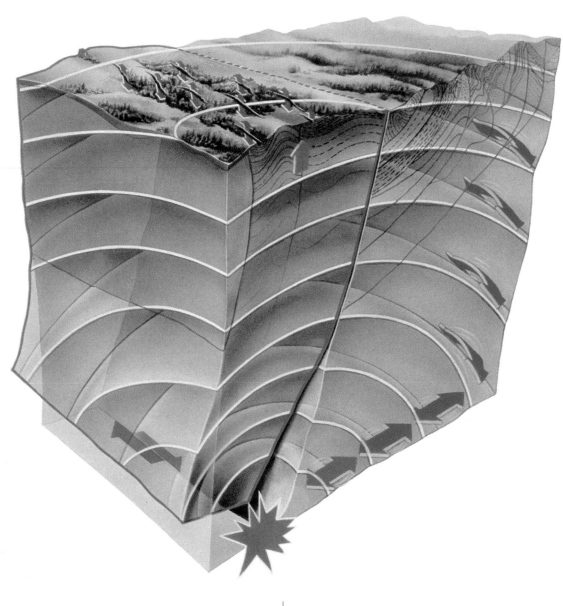

Right, the dark vertical line illustrates the location of a fault. As two plates grind against each other along the fault, strain increases in the Earth's crust. Eventually the crust snaps and moves, far right, releasing energy along the fault and causing an earthquake.

Opposite, the San Andreas Fault crosses the Carrizo Plain some 100 miles north of Los Angeles. One of the world's great seismic faults, the San Andreas extends almost the entire length of California. The surrounding landscape consists of pressure ridges formed as a result of hundreds of fault movements.

ing than the whim of supreme beings, early scientists attempted to fit earthquakes and volcanoes into their conception of the planet's structure. Aristotle, like many of his contemporaries, believed a fire burned deep within Earth. When winds from the atmosphere were drawn underground, they mixed with the central flames and then exploded upward toward the surface in convulsive earthquakes and volcanic blasts. With the discovery of electricity in the eighteenth century, Benjamin Franklin and others of his time speculated that earthquakes could stem from some sort of spark underground, much like lightning in the clouds overhead.

Still, even in the Age of Enlightenment, many people interpreted natural disasters as a sign of God's wrath. When a large earthquake and fire leveled Lisbon in 1755, much of Europe blamed the catastrophe on the immoral and superstitious character of the Portuguese capital. Not only did Lisbon boast tremendous wealth, it also was the center of the dreaded Inquisition. It was no accident, said English clergymen, that a Protestant church survived intact while most others collapsed. In fact, the Palace of the Inquisition was one of the first to fall.

But why does the ground occasionally spasm and shake? Although theories of the planet have changed dramatically since the days of ancient Greece, modern geologists would agree with Aristotle's belief that upheavals of the Earth stem—at least indirectly—from underground heat. The grand concept that explains this link is the theory of plate tectonics, which revolutionized Earth sciences in the 1960s. The theory draws its name from the Greek word "tekton," meaning builder. It's an apt term for a process that has sculpted Earth's mountain ranges and carved the deep ocean basins.

According to plate-tectonic theory, Earth's outer shell—or lithosphere—is broken into 20 irregularly shaped patches, each about 60 miles

Right, a computer-generated map shows the distribution of earthquakes of magnitude 5.5 or greater from 1963 to 1987 in relation to tectonic plates around the world. Earthquakes on the west coast of the Americas frequently occur where the American, Nazca, Cocos, and Pacific plates collide. In Africa and north of India in the Himalayas, though, this seismic correlation is not as evident.

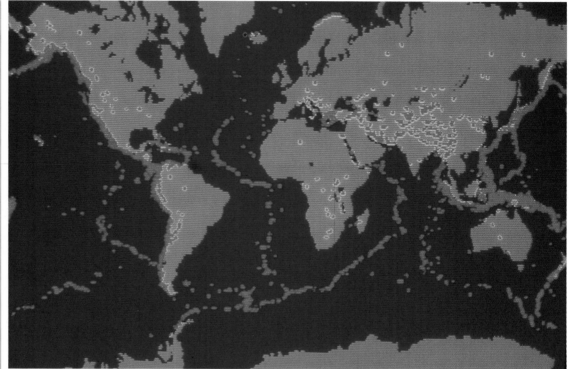

Above, a "black smoker," a sea-bottom hydrothermal vent, shoots out water rich in hydrogen sulfide along the East Pacific Rise, the juncture at which the Pacific and Nazca plates meet.

Opposite, artistic rendition of our constantly self-renewing Earth: along spreading zones on the ocean floor where the crust is thinnest, upwelling molten rock, churned by heat from the Earth's core, drives apart the crustal plates that ride on the upper mantle. When plates collide, either mountains are produced as one plate plunges under another (right corner) or the plates slide against, or pull away from, each other, creating fault lines. In either event, earthquakes and much ground displacement occur.

thick and hundreds to thousands of miles wide. The continents are embedded in these plates, which float upon a viscous layer of hot rock inside the planet's mantle.

The plates drift around the planet like bumper cars, constantly colliding and separating at speeds of an inch or two a year—about as fast as a fingernail grows. The force driving all this motion lies deep inside the planet. Internal heat creates swirling currents in the mantle that push the plates around the globe in endless motion. The hidden heat engine ultimately bears the blame for earthquakes and volcanoes.

When two plates crash together, the lithosphere buckles and bends, pushing up jagged mountain peaks. Over the last 40 million years, India has raised Mount Everest and the rest of the Himalayas by smashing head-on into Asia. Each year, the mountains inch higher as India rams farther northward. And when the world's tallest mountains grow, the crust beneath them cracks and quakes.

In other parts of the world, one plate will slide beneath another as it dives into the mantle. Aside from causing tremors and volcanic explosions, this process creates the deep ocean trenches—the lowest spots on Earth's surface.

Plates can also move past each other horizontally, like two trains heading in opposite directions. This is the case in California, which straddles the boundary between the Pacific plate and the North American plate. The infamous San Andreas Fault forms the junction between these two giant patches of Earth. A person standing to the west of the fault, say in Los Angeles, rides the Pacific plate in a slow but inexorable journey toward Alaska. On the eastern side of the fault, the North American plate inches south toward the equator.

The Pacific creeps past North America at an average speed of about a foot per decade. At that rate, Los Angeles will sidle up next to San Francisco in 20 million years.

Because of their rough edges, the plates don't glide smoothly against each other. Imagine rubbing two pieces of sandpaper together. The

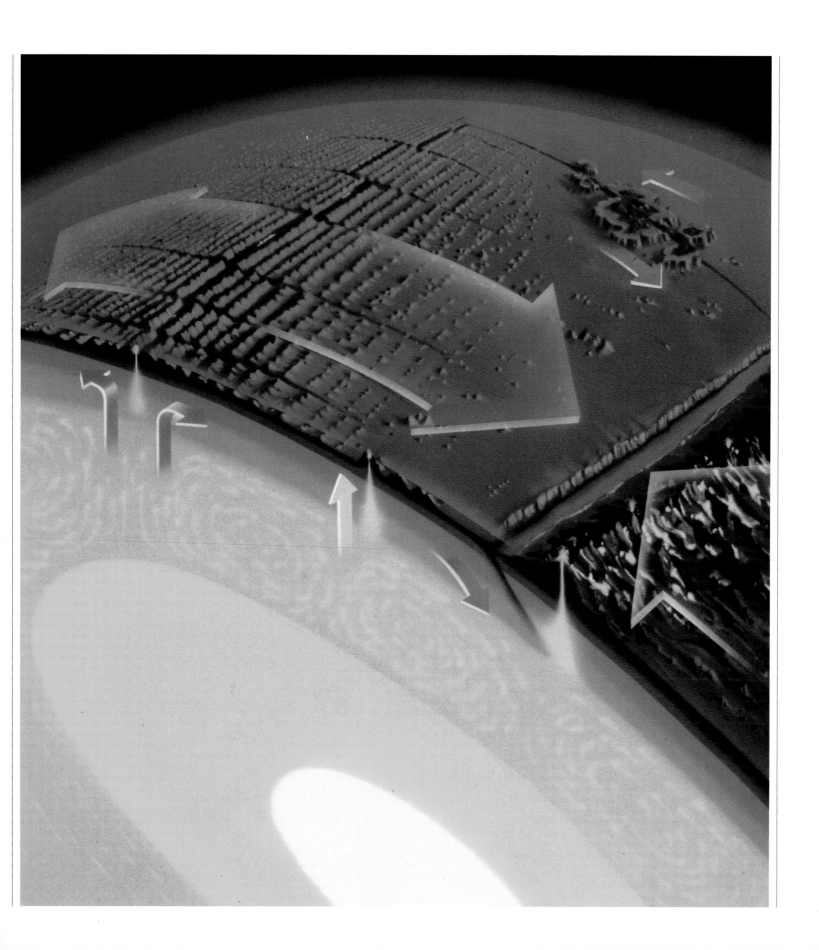

A MOST DEADLY DAY

A magnitude 7.8 earthquake flattened the city of Tangshan, China, on July 28, 1976, killing at least 250,000 people.

On July 27, 1976, the sky above Tangshan, China, burst with flashing lights, but no holiday justified the unusual fireworks. Luminous rays as colorful as the rainbow streamed over parts of the city in an inexplicable and disquieting display.

At around 3 A.M. the next morning, more flashes lit the sky and a loud noise roared through Tangshan, waking up some residents. Then a little before 4 A.M., the city of a million people ceased to exist.

Seismic waves from a massive earthquake shook Tangshan with forces far exceeding the pull of gravity. The vibrations slammed thousands of people into their ceilings before shattering their homes. Within seconds, 93 percent of the residential structures and 78 percent of the industrial buildings collapsed on hundreds of thousands of heads.

One school teacher mistook the pre-quake noises for a storm and ran outside to cover some of his possessions. As the shaking started, he cried "Earthquake" and tried to return to his family. Here is his painful recollection of what happened next:

> I heard a noise like a car screeching to a stop. Then I saw my house twisting from southeast to northwest and [it] shook once or twice before the roof and walls were thrown toward the northwest. I was also thrown 4 or 5 meters [13 to 16 feet] away. When I struggled to my feet, all the houses in front of me had collapsed.

Falling buildings immediately crushed thousands of people. But most of the disaster's victims survived the initial shock, only to suffocate after hours and days trapped amid the dusty wreckage. Chinese officials estimate that 250,000 people perished, whereas western observers put the death toll as high as 750,000.

The Tangshan earthquake measured magnitude 7.8, making this one of the largest recorded earthquakes to strike the middle of a tectonic plate—which generally is more stable than the plate edge. The main jolt hit with the strength of 400 atomic bombs of the size dropped on Hiroshima. Later in the day, a magnitude 7.1 aftershock finished off most of the buildings that had survived the initial attack.

Besides its tremendous size, the Tangshan tremor wrought so much damage because it caught Chinese scientists by surprise. No large earthquake had shaken the area in at least six centuries, so seismologists judged that Tangshan faced only moderate seismic risks. As a result, buildings were not constructed to the highest standards.

A year earlier, Chinese scientists had saved thousands of lives by predicting a major quake near the city of Haicheng in Manchuria. But Earth gave no clear warning in the weeks and days before the Tangshan quake. ∎

plates get snagged on uneven spots and remain locked together for decades, even centuries, as pressure slowly builds. Then, in a few fatal moments, the snag gives way.

On April 18, 1906, residents of San Francisco found out what happens when the crust can't take the strain anymore. At 5:12 A.M. the North American and Pacific plates jerked free along a 250-mile-long stretch of the San Andreas Fault. The plates lurched forward as much as 20 feet in some places, generating tremors of magnitude 8.2.

The 1906 disaster entered the history books as the Great San Francisco Earthquake, but this wasn't the first shock to earn that title. In 1868, the Hayward Fault south of Oakland, California, produced a strong temblor that damaged San Francisco as well as communities east of the bay. In San Francisco, the shaking in 1868 took the greatest toll on made ground—parts of the bay that had been filled. After the quake, many people suggested that construction on such reclaimed land be limited. Unfortunately, the city quickly forgot the lessons of the 1868 quake and faced the exact same problems with made ground in the 1906 disaster.

In the years that followed, San Franciscans once again ignored what they had learned. Using rubble from the very buildings that collapsed in 1906, the city filled in a lagoon along its north shore to create space for the Panama-Pacific International Exhibition of 1912. This area later evolved into the Marina district, an attractive site to build homes.

Nature does not indulge forgetfulness, however. The Loma Prieta earthquake in 1989 hammered the Marina district and other regions underlain by fill, demonstrating yet again the hazards of building on weak ground.

Residents of San Francisco and neighboring cities may soon have to face another rude shock, according to quake experts. Seismologists have calculated that the Bay Area has a two-in-three chance of suffering a magnitude 7 quake by the year 2020.

NO SAFE GROUND

Although most earthquakes strike along the restless edges of tectonic plates, interior lands are not immune to damaging jolts. In fact, the strongest series of shocks in the contiguous United States broke not in California, but in the nation's heartland. During the winter of 1811-1812, three great tremors considered larger than magnitude 8 reared up from the Missouri boot heel and raced out across the continent.

The seismic storm hit at a stressful time in the history of the young nation. Less than 30 years after a taxing struggle to win independence, the United States in 1811 was again bracing for war with England. Across the center of the country, U.S. troops battled an army of Native Americans united under the Shawnee leader Tecumseh. The Shawnee and other tribes had grown desperate, foreseeing the eventual destruction of their way of life. Tecumseh channeled their anger into a nationalistic movement that flared briefly before meeting its demise at the battle of Tippecanoe, Indiana, in November 1811.

Tecumseh actually missed that fight, having traveled south into Alabama to gather support from communities there. According to legend, Tecumseh grew angry when a local Creek leader challenged his authority. The great Shawnee chief departed, vowing to destroy all the houses in the Creek village by stamping his foot upon arriving in Detroit. Day after day, the Creeks anxiously waited. On the morning they calculated that Tecumseh would reach Detroit, the land began to tremble and all the Creek houses fell. The first New Madrid earthquake had struck.

The tale of Tecumseh's prophecy is myth. But the trio of terrible quakes and hundreds of strong aftershocks left indelible marks on the

landscape and in historical records. On December 16, the first of the earthquakes unleashed such violent tremors that it woke people in Washington, D.C., 750 miles away from the epicenter. With water pitchers rattling and curtains swaying, many Washingtonians thought that burglars had broken into their homes.

On January 23, the New Madrid region let loose a second massive burst of energy, followed 15 days later by the greatest shock of all. Over half the United States felt the vibrations from this quake, which tore down chimneys and cracked brick walls as far away as Cincinnati, more than 300 miles distant.

The epicentral region, however, suffered the most from these shocks. Godfrey Le Sieur, a young boy near Caruthersville, Missouri, described how the ground heaved and eventually exploded around him: "The earth was observed to be rolling in waves of a few feet in height, with a visible depression between. By and by these swells burst, throwing up large volumes of water, sand and a species of charcoal."

The quakes warped the land so much that some parts of the Mississippi River ran backwards for a few hours and waterfalls appeared temporarily. On land, geysers of sand and coal erupted from the ground, leaving thousands of craters pockmarking the region. Dust in the air darkened the sky, making the sun glow an angry red. Everywhere, sulfurous fumes assaulted the senses. For many people, especially lax churchgoers, it seemed that the Day of Judgment had arrived, turning the once prosperous land into a punishing hell.

At first glance, the theory of plate tectonics seems powerless to explain such quakes. Geologists typically expect tremors in California, Alaska, and other places where two plates crunch together. These geologically active areas, after all, are often laced with abundant faults. But the New Madrid area lies in the seemingly stable center of the North American plate, more than 1,000 miles from the nearest plate boundary.

To resolve the paradox, scientists have performed the modern equivalent of Tecumseh's heavy-footed stomping. Seismologists thump the ground with small explosions or special trucks and then record how the seismic waves bounce off hidden geologic structures. Although no active faults are visible at the surface, geophysicists have discovered major fractures several miles underground.

The buried faults formed as much as 500 million years ago, when the forces of plate tectonics began to pull North America apart. A great rift opened up in the New Madrid area, threatening to split the continent in two. Eventually, the incipient fissure stopped growing and the wound healed. But the scars of that episode have weakened the crust in the middle of North America, leaving faults that occasionally unleash strong earthquakes.

According to geological evidence, the New Madrid area has several times in the past few thousand years suffered major jolts. Should another magnitude 8 occur soon, scientists say, it would instantly devastate the Mississippi Valley from Memphis to St. Louis. Cities as far away as Dallas and Chicago could suffer serious effects. In some scenarios, casualty estimates range in the thousands and the damage exceeds $50 billion.

Because such massive quakes recur every 550 to 1,100 years or more, many centuries may pass before the next one reroutes the Mississippi. The central United States, however, shouldn't put off seismic preparations. Quakes in the range of magnitude 6 to magnitude 7 have ripped the New Madrid region every 90 years or so and will cause considerable damage when the next one strikes. The last such jolt occurred in 1895, leading seismologists to expect another sometime in the next few decades.

Scientists say there is a 60 percent chance that

a damaging quake will surface somewhere east of the Rocky Mountains in the next two decades. In all, 39 states stand a significant chance of suffering a strong shock in the future. But because most eastern states have no seismic construction codes or are just beginning to establish them, any sizable quake could take a tremendous toll on weak buildings. Making matters even worse, the crust in this part of the country is relatively unfractured, so it transmits seismic waves well—unlike the broken, absorbent crust of California. For that reason, an earthquake in the East can damage an area many times larger than a similar jolt in California.

Past events have demonstrated the wide-reaching power of eastern quakes. In 1755, a magnitude 6 tremor occurred in the Atlantic Ocean off the coast of Massachusetts. Despite the distance

Above, contract workers for the California Department of Transportation finished repairs only a month after the collapse of the San Francisco-Oakland Bay Bridge due to an October 17, 1989, earthquake.

Opposite, only one person died when an upper section of the San Francisco-Oakland Bay Bridge collapsed during the 1989 earthquake and plunged the car into the quake-formed chasm. The structural stress relieved by this rupture helped to prevent any further damage to the bridge, as well as any additional deaths.

SAN FRANCISCO: APRIL 18, 1906

Above, the intensity of the quake was amplified in some areas where the city was built on landfill.

Opposite, following the historic earthquake of 1906, San Franciscans gathered on a hill overlooking the city to watch as smoke and fire engulfed it.

The faint hues of dawn were creeping across the sky when the first shock rocked San Francisco. For the 400,000 residents wrenched from sleep, no nightmare could have rivaled the scene they encountered. Fred J. Hewitt, a reporter for the San Francisco Examiner, described what he saw on the street near City Hall:

It is impossible to judge the length of that shock. To me it seemed an eternity. I was thrown...on my back and the pavement pulsated like a living thing. Around me the huge buildings looming up were terrible because of the queer dance they were performing....Crash following crash resounded on all sides. Screeches rent the air as terrified humanity streamed out

into the open in an agony of despair. Frightened horses dashed headlong into ruins as they raced away in their abject fear.

The quake came in two installments, starting with a tremor of roughly 20 seconds. Then the more violent main shock attacked for some 45 to 60 seconds, collapsing an untold number of buildings around the city. The areas hardest hit were those on made ground—coves, swamps, and other low-lying regions that had been filled in with garbage, loose soil, wood, and even old ships discarded after the Gold Rush.

The great opera tenor, Enrico Caruso, was sleeping in the Palace Hotel at the time of the quake, having finished a performance of *Carmen* only hours before. People later saw the star wearing a fur coat over his pajamas, vowing never to return to the city.

For San Franciscans, the great earthquake marked only the start of the disaster. Minutes after the first

tremors subsided, fires erupted and started to spread through the crippled city. The blazes had a variety of causes, from downed electrical wires to toppled stoves and severed gas lines. One particularly destructive conflagration started later in the morning and is remembered as the Ham and Egg Fire. It began in Hayes Valley when a hungry woman tried to cook some breakfast, which quickly set her earthquake-damaged chimney aflame.

Firefighters tried to battle the Hayes Valley blaze and others around the city. But their efforts were doomed from the start. The fire department suffered a serious blow in the first minutes of the quake when bricks from the California Hotel crashed through a neighboring fire station. Sleeping inside was department chief Dennis T. Sullivan, who received extensive injuries from which he died three days later.

Even without their respected leader, the firefighters of San Francisco might have saved their city if not for a second problem. When

the squads went to tap the fire hydrants, they found that the quake had severed most of the city's water mains. In desperation, the firemen blew up buildings with dynamite to make fire breaks—a tactic that in many instances worsened the inferno.

When the writer Jack London wrote about the fire for *Collier's* magazine, he described a surreal scene as seen from San Francisco Bay:

It was dead calm. Not a flicker of wind stirred. Yet from every side, wind was pouring in upon the city. East, west, north, and south, strong winds were blowing upon the doomed city. The heated air rising made an enormous suck. Thus did the fire of itself build its own colossal chimney through the atmosphere. Day and night the dead calm continued, and yet, near to the flames, the wind was often half a gale...

In 1906, San Francisco was a city just waiting to burn. Only a year ear-

lier, the National Board of Fire Underwriters had reported that the congested narrow streets, poor construction, lack of sprinklers, and hilly topography greatly increased the risk of uncontrollable conflagrations. The board concluded:

In fact, San Francisco has violated all underwriting traditions and precedents by not burning up; that it has not done so is largely due to the vigilance of the fire department, which can not be relied upon indefinitely to stave off the inevitable.

A year later, the fire fulfilled the board's prophecy. When the smoke finally cleared three days after the great earthquake, San Francisco lay in ruins. The entire business district and 60 percent of the residential buildings in the city had burned. More than 2,593 acres had gone up in smoke. Four hundred and ninety city blocks were destroyed completely, and 32 burned in part. With whole neighborhoods reduced to smoldering rubble, San Francisco looked like it

Above, the charred remains of buildings that withstood the 1906 San Francisco Earthquake only to be consumed by three days of ensuing fires.

had suffered a nuclear attack.

Suddenly finding themselves homeless, hundreds of thousands of people fled the city by train or ferry in the greatest evacuation of any U.S. city during peacetime. Thousands of other unfortunate souls remained in San Francisco, huddling in makeshift camps. Many had lost everything—possessions, children, spouses. One lament tacked on a wall typified signs that adorned the city:

The cow is in the hammock
The cat is in the lake
The baby in the garbage can,
What difference does it make?
There is no water,
    and still less soap
We have no city, but lots of hope.

Until recently, historians have repeated old reports that 700 people died in the earthquake and fire. Researchers now believe the actual death toll reached 2,500 to 3,000. ■

Top left, the burned-out shell of the $7 million city hall building towers over widespread desolation.

Top right, the rippling motion of the quake twisted cable-car lines and heaved up brick-covered Union Street.

Center, refugees patiently await their turn at one of dozens of relief centers set up around the city.

Left, a family prepares dinner on the streets of San Francisco. Resilient San Franciscans resumed their daily activities outdoors as many buildings were either demolished or rendered uninhabitable by the quake.

Right, rescuers try to reach people trapped in collapsed buildings during the magnitude 7.8 earthquake that shook Mexico City on September 19, 1985.

Above, pain and agony are etched on the face of this rescue worker. Right, the remains of an unfortunate victim trapped beneath the Mexico City rubble.

Opposite, rescuers search the collapsed ruins of Juarez Hospital in Mexico City.

and its moderate strength, the quake knocked down walls and chimneys in Boston. People felt the tremor across a 400,000-square-mile region, from Nova Scotia to the Chesapeake Bay.

Seismologists can't tell where the next eastern quake will strike. They can only look at previous tremors for hints of impending ones. Strong quakes have rocked Pennsylvania, Ohio, Virginia, and even New York City, which suffered a magnitude 5 shock in 1884. One can imagine how the older tenements in Manhattan would fare during even a modest quake.

Residents of Charleston, South Carolina, need not wonder what will happen to the stately homes in their city. History provides a vivid illustration.

Throughout the summer of 1886, people in Charleston and surrounding areas had largely ignored the small tremors that shook the city. After all, they had suffered enough ill fortune in the Civil War and its aftermath; what could a few inconsequential shakes do? Charleston was just beginning to blossom again as a center of commerce and of the performing arts. An editorial that year in the *News and Courier* sang the town's praises: "Nature has done everything she possibly could for Charleston."

But nature had more in store for the city. On August 31, even as a work crew finished repairing recent hurricane damage to the steeple of St. Michael's Church, the ground started lurching violently, sending 14,000 chimneys tumbling to the ground. Collapsing buildings killed 110 people and injured scores of others.

Like the New Madrid quake and many others, the magnitude 7.5 Charleston disaster struck in what might otherwise seem stable land far from any plate boundary. But seismologists think that old wounds in the crust underlie Charleston, just as they do New Madrid. Clearly this region also has the potential to produce strong tremors in the future.

MONSTER QUAKES

For all their destructive power, the Charleston
and New Madrid jolts pale when compared to
the planet's mightiest earthquakes, which sur-
pass magnitude 9. These monsters tear such
large patches of Earth's surface that they set the
entire globe ringing like a bell for weeks on end.

The most recent mammoth tremor ravaged
southern Alaska on March 27, 1964. That day,
Good Friday, started out quietly enough. In
Anchorage, snow fell intermittently throughout
the day, but the temperature reached a high of
38 degrees Fahrenheit, balmy conditions for
Alaska in the first week of spring. By 5 P.M.,
people who hadn't been given the day off were
making their way home from work.

Residents of Anchorage and surrounding
towns considered themselves old hands when it
came to earthquakes. Small tremors frequently
rattled the region, and people knew what to
expect from these minor jolts. Larger quakes
didn't seem to present a problem; no one could
remember any damaging shocks.

That string of good fortune ended at 5:36
P.M. Twelve miles beneath the coast of Prince
William Sound, a stuck patch of the Pacific
crust suddenly jerked 60 feet northwest, generating an intense seismic storm that remains the
strongest North American earthquake ever
recorded. Seventy-five thousand square miles
of ocean rock scraped against an equal area of
continental crust, producing wave after wave of
tremors. The convulsions emanating from this
fault had such power that they caused the
ground to bulge up to two inches as they raced
unnoticed through Chicago, Boston, and other
parts of the United States. Even after crossing
the globe, the vibrations had enough punch to
upset water levels in South African wells.

In the earthquake's backyard, those same
seismic waves terrorized the residents of coastal
Alaska for four long minutes. The extended

Top, in the town of Spitak, Armenia, thousands of coffins stockpiled in the stadium await those killed by the magnitude 6.9 earthquake that nearly leveled the town on December 7, 1988.

A soldier, above, rests on his shovel, weary from his efforts to free trapped victims. Right, a child's doll lies among the ruins of an apartment building.

Opposite, a family in the town of Leninakan, Armenia, grieves over the loss of their son.

shaking turned the solid soil beneath Anchorage into Jell-O. Massive landslides resulted, sweeping away homes and buildings. Downtown along Fourth Avenue, two and a half blocks of stores, shops, and other businesses sank until their entrances came to rest below street level. A landslide also tore apart the fashionable suburb of Turnagain Heights, where some residents ran out of their shaking homes only to be swallowed by yawning crevasses in the ground.

Although collapsing buildings killed several people, the ocean claimed most of the 115 Alaskan victims. Almost instantly after the quake, large waves triggered by landslides began to hammer coastal communities.

In Seward, Alaska, the waves caught fire after picking up oil spilled from ruptured storage tanks. A number of residents raced for their lives with flaming water at their heels. Men dove under bouncing railroad cars and leapt over fissures as they ran for higher ground. A wave hit the oil tanker, *Alaska Standard*, washing away Ted Pedersen, who stood on a dock below his ship. When he regained consciousness, Pedersen was sprawled on the tanker's catwalk eight feet above the deck.

Twenty minutes later, even more massive waves called tsunamis struck the entire coastline from Kodiak Island to Prince William Sound. These black walls of water, up to 40 feet high, steamed through Resurrection Bay and crashed into Seward, engulfing houses, railroad cars, airplanes, and hangars. Some people who could not escape to higher ground survived by climbing trees or scrambling onto rooftops only moments before the waves swept past.

On Kodiak Island, Karl Armstrong fled town but came back after the first tsunami, not realizing that more would strike. When other people yelled that a second one was on the way, Armstrong ran to a nearby hill with the giant

wave in pursuit. He recalled the close encounter for investigators who visited Kodiak months later:

You could hear it. You didn't know where it was, but you could actually hear it coming. It...literally poured over the breakwater and into the boat harbor. The boat harbor all of a sudden was higher than the town. You could see all the boats riding high up in the air. Then they moved...right into town.

Residents of Crescent City, California, didn't have Armstrong's luck. Three and one-half hours after the Alaskan quake, this town received word that a tsunami was headed its way. The sheriff sent deputies to alert people living near the ocean. At midnight, a mild first wave arrived as scheduled. A second followed at 12:40 A.M. and a third at 1:20 A.M. If the waves had stopped there, the city would have escaped largely unscathed. But the last wave—a 20-foot-tall giant—hit much harder than the preceding three. It washed away 11 people who had returned to clean up damage from the earlier swells.

The same waves killed four people along the Oregon coast and pounded boats in San Francisco Bay. They eventually lapped against the icy coastline of Antarctica at the other end of the globe.

The Alaskan quake had a magnitude of 9.2 and released roughly 5,000 times the energy of the 1994 jolt in Northridge. But the Good Friday quake can't claim first place in the record books. That goes to a giant earthquake that devastated Chile on May 22, 1960. Seismologists have calculated that this quake had a magnitude of 9.5 and unleashed energy equal to one-quarter of the world's nuclear arsenal. The earthquake killed thousands of people in Chile and spawned a tsunami that claimed 61 lives in Hawaii, 120 in Japan, and more than 20 in the Philippines.

In terms of plate tectonics, the Chilean and Alaskan quakes are siblings. They both occurred

Above, the magnitude 9.2 Alaska earthquake of 1964, the strongest ever recorded in North America, ignited oil tanks that produced a towering plume of black smoke, left, visible for many miles.

Opposite, a fissure caused by the 1964 Alaska earthquake dissected this school on Government Hill in Anchorage.

TERROR FROM THE SEA

Residents of Hilo, Hawaii, flee the onrushing fury of a tsunami on April 1, 1946.

The citizens of Hilo, Hawaii, couldn't believe their eyes on April 1, 1946. All the water had drained out of the three-mile-wide bay, leaving hundreds of fish floundering on the exposed seafloor.

Hilo didn't have to wait long for an answer. Within moments, a giant wave thundered into the empty bay. It slammed into a row of seaside buildings and carried them effortlessly across the street. With a giant sucking sound, the water then retreated from Hilo Bay, carrying with it an armada of debris and several people. A second wave crashed into the city, then a third. Hilo lost 96 souls that day; 63 more perished in other parts of Hawaii.

The cause of Hilo's misfortune lay in the Aleutian Islands 2,200 miles to the north. Five hours earlier, a magnitude 7.3 earthquake had jacked up a section of the seafloor, displacing enough water to create a tsunami.

These gigantic waves are practically invisible as they race through the open ocean, but when they reach shallow water, they can rear up to great heights, forming walls of water that pound coastal towns. Traveling at 500 miles per hour, tsunamis cross the Pacific in less than a day. And they lose little power in transit.

The word tsunami means "harbor wave" in Japanese, a fitting term because these killers don't show their true nature until they come close to shore. Moving into shallow water, the front of the tsunami slows down while the back of the wave keeps racing forward. That action piles up a mountain of water steaming toward shore. These killers are often called tidal waves in English, but tsunamis have no connection with the tides. While seafloor earthquakes spawn most tsunamis, volcanic blasts can also trigger them. In 1883, an eruption of Krakatau in Indonesia generated waves up to 130 feet high that leveled 165 coastal villages and killed at least 36,000 people. ∎

in places where a slab of ocean crust collides with a continent and dives underneath. As the oceanic plate pushes into the Earth, it gets hung up temporarily on rough edges beneath the continent. The two plates remain locked together, building up stress over the years until they finally jerk free in a great burst of seismic energy.

This process, called subduction, is currently consuming ocean crust all around the Pacific Rim. And almost everywhere that one plate grinds beneath another, large quakes are bound to follow. Japan, Indonesia, Central America, and western South America, among other spots, suffer the consequences of sitting above a subducting plate.

In 1985, Mexico City also learned the dangers of subduction, even though this inland metropolis sits a full 200 miles from the nearest shore. On September 19, a magnitude 8.1 earthquake broke beneath the Pacific seafloor, sending seismic waves racing toward the mountain-rimmed valley that holds the city. Although the vibrations weakened considerably during the 60-second journey, when they reached Mexico City, they shook the sediment-filled valley in such a way that the land amplified the tremors. Hundreds of buildings located on this sandy soil collapsed, killing 9,500 people.

In recent years, scientists have discovered that large subduction quakes occasionally clobber the Pacific Northwest as well. None of these shocks has occurred in the last 200 years—the limit of recorded history in the region. But the coastlines of Washington and Oregon preserve clear evidence that such megajolts have hit in the past, most recently around the year 1680. Because geologists don't know how regularly these giant quakes strike, they can't tell when to expect the next one beneath Seattle and Portland.

When they look at the record for the entire globe, geologists calculate that truly great earthquakes wrack some spot on the planet every few

Page 157: Unlike wind-driven surface waves which normally dissipate after a few miles, tsunamis or "harbor waves," most commonly generated by earthquakes, extend all the way to the ocean floor and can travel thousands of miles without weakening.

Above, smoldering aerial view of destruction caused by a tsunami and fires in the Aonae district of Japan's Okushiri Island on July 13, 1993. The wave, originating from an earthquake in the Sea of Japan, washed over areas 97 feet above sea level and drowned or crushed to death 120 people.

Opposite, (left to right, top to bottom) computerized images composed at four-hour intervals beginning immediately after Chile's 1960 coastal earthquake, show the track of tsunamis as they race across the Pacific Ocean toward Japan. Tsunamis caused by the earthquake lasted for more than a week.

decades. But none has hit since 1964. Simple arithmetic says the next one could come anytime.

WHEN MOUNTAINS BREATHE FIRE

The clock read 2:10 P.M., but the ash-filled sky was pitch black when the order came to evacuate. An intrepid team of U.S. and Filipino volcanologists had manned its monitoring post as long as possible to keep tabs on Mount Pinatubo, 15 miles to the west. The scientists had saved countless lives in the last few days, but the erupting volcano now threatened their base. Avalanches of incandescent rock and gas were sweeping down the mountainside toward them, and no one knew how far the deadly flows would travel.

With gallows humor, scientist Andy Lockhart ran through the building telling people, "You'd better put jam in your pockets because we're about to become toast."

The crew retreated under a sky that dropped heavy, wet ash and pieces of pumice as large as golf balls. Soon, the ground shuddered with strong earthquakes. The shocks hit every 15 minutes or so as Pinatubo vomited pulverized rock and gases 22 miles into the air. Darkness reigned throughout the day until the mountain's rage finally weakened. "It was the closest thing to hell that I can ever describe," one scientist recalled.

Eighty years had passed since Earth witnessed an eruption of the size that wracked Mount Pinatubo on June 15, 1991. If all the rock and ash ejected from the Philippine volcano were dumped onto the island of Manhattan, it would bury the city under 1,000 feet of debris, leaving only the tallest skyscrapers peaking through the gray rubble.

After 500 years of slumber, Pinatubo had picked a particularly bad time to awaken. The blast occurred just as a typhoon blew over the

island of Luzon, passing only 30 miles north of the volcano. The double whammy of Typhoon Yunya and Pinatubo combined to kill more than 300 people, most of whom were crushed when rain-soaked ash caused the roofs of their buildings to collapse. Even after the eruption ceased, mudflows months later claimed hundreds of lives.

Yet the death toll could easily have reached into the tens of thousands, if not for the work of scientists who tracked the volcano's activity. Mount Pinatubo first showed signs of unrest in early April, when minor steam blasts coughed up small clouds of ash. Volcanologists from the Philippines set up a seismometer on the mountain and detected 200 volcanic quakes in the first 24 hours. Alarmed by the unrest, the scientists appealed to U.S. colleagues for assistance.

Two weeks later, a team of American experts arrived with seismometers and other instruments to help monitor the groaning peak. Convinced that Pinatubo would soon blow, the scientists and civil authorities successfully evacuated more than 58,000 people from the area before the volcano let fly.

The blast ejected so much debris into the atmosphere that it knocked the climate of the entire Earth out of kilter temporarily. More than 15 million tons of sulfurous gas reached the stratosphere, where it combined with water vapor to form tiny reflective droplets. Carried by swift winds, the volcanic acid particles circled the globe in three weeks, creating a veil that cut the amount of sunlight reaching the ground. This global umbrella depressed the planet's average temperature by a full degree Fahrenheit. It also helped chlorine pollution in the atmosphere chew away at the protective ozone shield.

While volcanologists averted a gruesome disaster at Pinatubo, their efforts had failed to prevent a tragedy six years earlier, when a Colombian giant called Nevado del Ruiz roared

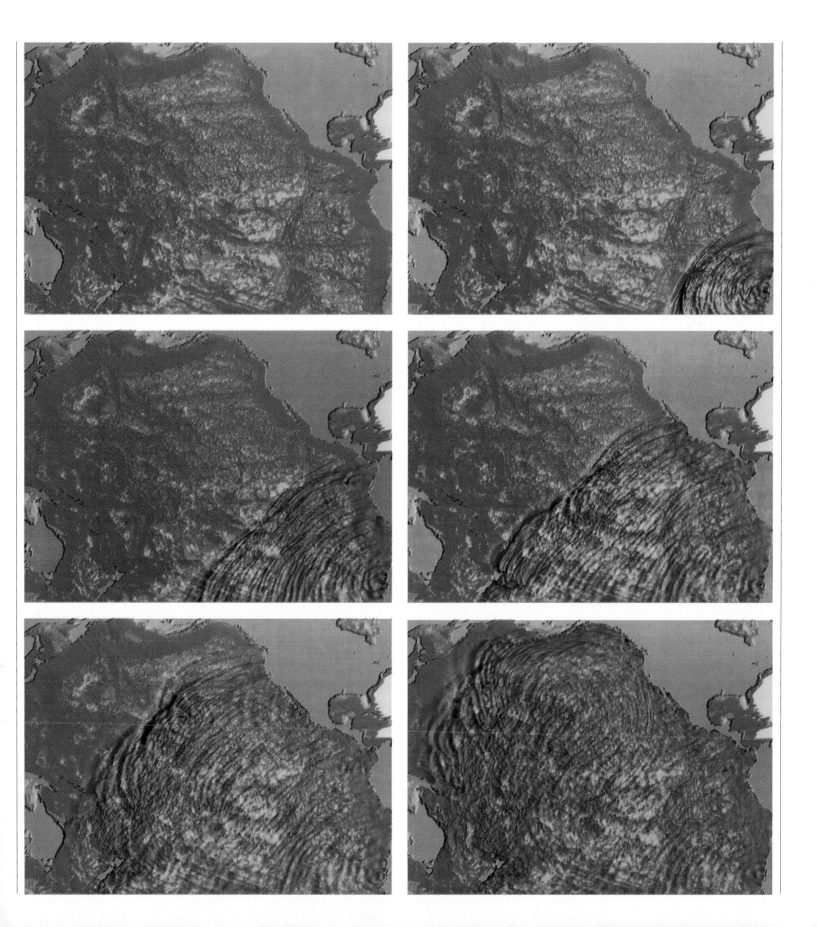

Right, molten rock, called magma, rises under tremendous pressure from a chamber beneath a volcano, releasing tons of ash and heated gases. The process by which one continental plate travels under another, bottom right, possibly creating volcanoes as it melts in the Earth's mantle, is called subduction.

Pages 160-161: Jets of lava from a January 1992 eruption of Sicily's Mount Etna light up the night sky. Widely viewed as destructive, volcanic eruptions release nutrient-rich elements—phosphorus, potassium, calcium, magnesium, and sulfur—vital to plant growth.

Pages 162-163: Artificial channels in the Valle del Bove (Valley of the Cows), just below the active vents of Mount Etna, divert searing hot lava flow from a village that lies in the lava's original path.

to life. During late 1984 and much of 1985, the ice-capped mountain quaked and let loose small eruptions, causing scientists to wonder whether a major blast was brewing. They cautioned that the town of Armero, population 29,000, faced a distinct risk because it rested directly on mud-flow deposits from former eruptions. In fact, murky torrents of ash and water had claimed 1,000 lives in that very same spot when Nevado del Ruiz last erupted in 1845.

But the scientists' clear warnings were never translated into life-saving action. Communication broke down between researchers and government officials, so critical information never reached the endangered populations. The mistakes had dire consequences. On November 13, 1985, small eruptions began in midafternoon and rained ash on Armero in the evening. Some people heeded the volcanic signs and left, but most listened to radio reports and public announcements that urged citizens to remain calm.

About 9 P.M., fresh molten rock started to shoot up through the volcano. As this magma exploded out of the crater, it melted snow and ice on top of Nevado del Ruiz. Two hours later, a river of mud one-fifth the size of the Amazon raced down the mountainside and out onto the plain below, instantly entombing 22,000 souls in Armero and surrounding regions.

Though relatively small in geologic terms, the 1985 explosion at Nevado del Ruiz took a ghastly toll. The disaster extinguished more lives than any other volcanic eruption in this century, with the exception of the tragedy that befell the Caribbean island of Martinique in 1902.

Like the Colombian incident, the catastrophe on Martinique need not have occurred. For weeks before the main eruption, Mount Pelée had rattled the citizens of nearby St. Pierre with small earthquakes and minor clouds of ash. On May 5, boiling mud coursed down the volcano,

Left, the most powerful eruptions pump fine ash and gases into the upper atmosphere. Jet streams spread this matter around the globe, often with widespread effects on weather and climate. A planetary haze may temporarily reduce temperatures before natural forces cleanse the pall. A monster eruption in 1815 of Mount Tambora in Indonesia was followed by a cool and highly irregular summer throughout the Northern Hemisphere.

Three-toed horses, *Pliohippis* and *Teleoceras*, struggle to breathe in this artist's reconstruction of a volcanic ashfall 10 million years ago in what is now Nebraska. Originating perhaps 1,000 miles away, the cloud came from an eruption 100 times as powerful as Mount St. Helens'.

More than a dozen adult and young extinct rhinos were among the 200 fossil skeletons, left, unearthed from glassy ash by a University of Nebraska State Museum crew near the town of Orchard during the 1970s.

MOUNT VESUVIUS

Jean-Baptiste Génillion (1750-1829) painted the fury of Mount Vesuvius, above.

Below right, these Romans found their final resting place when Herculaneum was buried by a volcanic mudflow from Vesuvius.

Vesuvius is the world's best known volcano. Much of its fame is due to a great eruption on August 24, A.D. 79 which disgorged mud-like avalanches of burning gases and glowing solids toward nearby Pompeii and Herculaneum.

Moving downhill at about 60 miles per hour, the result was nature's napalm. People at nearby Herculaneum were stopped in their tracks, some buried by up to 65 feet of debris. Miles away in Pompeii, victims were suffocated by volcanic gases two hours before an ash flow covered their corpses.

A remarkable description of the event was written by Pliny the Younger, the 18-year-old nephew of Pliny the Elder, a noted natural historian who died when his curiosity took him too close to the volcano. "Mount Vesuvius was blazing in several places," the young scribe recalled, while "a black and dreadful cloud bursting out in gusts of igneous serpentine vapour now and again yawned open to reveal long, fantastic flames, resembling flashes of lightning but much larger."

Today, the communities destroyed by the A.D. 79 eruption lie within the greater metropolitan area of Naples, Italy, with some two million inhabitants. Quiet since 1944, Vesuvius is not dead but only sleeps. It will surely awaken again. ■

killing a few dozen people at a sugar mill, two miles north of the city.

Citizens in St. Pierre grew alarmed and some sought to leave. But an important election was scheduled for May 10. Not wanting to lose votes in the city, the governor played down the volcanic risk. He even used soldiers to stop people from fleeing town.

At 7:50 A.M. on May 8, Mount Pelée curtailed the governor's reelection campaign. Red-hot pyroclastic flows—a froth of searing gases and ash—roared down the mountain at 120 miles per hour. Hugging the ground, the incandescent cloud blasted through St. Pierre with temperatures exceeding 1,000 degrees Fahrenheit.

The glowing avalanche ripped the city's buildings apart and snuffed out almost every living creature. Out of a population of 29,000 people, only two survived. One of them, a man named Auguste Ciparis, was serving time in a windowless dungeon when the inferno blazed through town. Rescue workers finally reached Ciparis three days later, finding him badly burned but still alive.

Because of their speed and tremendous temperatures, pyroclastic flows are one of the most dangerous features of a volcanic eruption. They often develop when a rising ash cloud grows too heavy and collapses on itself. The dense, glowing currents then run along the ground like a torrent from hell. Pyroclastic flows can also form when rapidly expanding magma bubbles out of a volcanic vent and falls down a mountainside.

It was pyroclastic flows that annihilated the cities of Pompeii and Herculaneum during the eruption of Italy's Mount Vesuvius in A.D. 79. For hours at the start of the disaster, ash and pumice fell on Pompeii, giving some people time to escape. But Vesuvius then served up glowing avalanches too swift to outrun. The flows entombed the two cities and thousands of

Page 167: The ruins of ancient Pompeii repose in the shadow of an enormous, two-mile-wide crater carved out by the explosion of Mount Vesusvius in A.D. 79.

Suzanne Christiansen, top, watches Mount St. Helens from Mount Adams, 35 miles away on May 18, 1980. At 8:32 A.M., above, an earthquake knocked Suzanne off her feet as it toppled Mount St. Helens' north slope, sending half a cubic mile of debris into the valley in 37 seconds.

Opposite, Washington's Mount St. Helens loses 1,300 feet of its peak, blasting 275 million tons of earth skyward. Fifty-seven people died or disappeared in the ash and rubble of the volcano.

people in deposits that reached 65 feet deep in some places.

Roman naturalist Pliny the Elder went to investigate the eruption of Vesuvius, but his curiosity was his downfall. His nephew, Pliny the Younger, described how the corpulent man collapsed and died in the heat of the moment.

DANGER IN THE NEIGHBORHOOD

At the time of Vesuvius' eruption, the science of volcanology was in its infancy. In his 37-volume encyclopedia *Natural History*, Pliny the Elder described the active volcanoes known at the time, which could be counted on the fingers of two hands. Scientists today recognize over 1,300 volcanoes that have erupted in the last 10,000 years and therefore are considered active.

Even at this moment, some 15 volcanoes are erupting in major or minor fashion somewhere around the globe. Chances are high that at least one of them can be found in the United States, which has more historically active volcanoes than any nation other than Indonesia and Japan. Over half of the 165 U.S. volcanoes are located in Alaska and the Aleutian Islands, far from cities and towns. But even the contiguous 48 states have 70 mountains capable of blowing.

Those who live in the shadows of these restless peaks don't always recognize the potential danger in their neighborhoods. The people of southwestern Washington, for example, did not wonder what created the symmetrical snow-capped cone rising above the conifer forests along the Columbia River. They did not know that Native Americans had long refused to live near the *Louwala Clough*, or smoking mountain. Recent arrivals in the area knew the peak only by its new name, Mount St. Helens.

On March 20, 1980, the volcano started to reveal its true nature when a magnitude 4.2 earthquake popped beneath it. After a 123-year

slumber, Mount St. Helens was coming awake. A swarm of earthquakes followed that initial jolt, and a minor eruption jetted ash and steam into the air a week later. Over the next seven weeks, St. Helens frequently ejected clouds of debris while it trembled with 10,000 small quakes. At the same time, a large bulge developed on the north flank of the mountain, pushed out by fresh magma rising under the volcano. The hump swelled at the astounding rate of five feet per day, signaling an eruption was imminent.

With advice from scientists monitoring St. Helens, Washington Governor Dixy Lee Ray blocked access to the mountain, angering people who owned cabins near Spirit Lake, less than five miles from the volcano. One of the dissenters, a headstrong 84-year-old named Harry Truman, refused to leave the mountain he had called home for half a century. Truman quickly became a celebrity, telling reporters that the volcano would never harm his property.

On May 18, the sun rose into clear skies over Mount St. Helens. From his campsite six miles to the north, volcanologist David A. Johnston of the U.S. Geological Survey measured the mountain's progress and radioed in his findings: Situation largely unchanged. To Johnston and other scientists, St. Helens seemed no more dangerous that morning than it had been for weeks. No harbinger announced the coming storm.

At 8:32 A.M, a magnitude 5.1 earthquake shook the volcano, destabilizing the bulging north flank. Those watching the mountain from a distance saw the north face grow fuzzy as it slowly started to collapse and slide downhill. Rippling and churning, the rock picked up speed, forming the largest avalanche ever witnessed. Within roughly a minute, 300 feet of volcanic rock had buried Harry Truman and his lodge.

For the magma trapped inside the volcano, the collapse of the mountain's flank was like

Researchers, above, use instruments to measure Mount St. Helens' lava dome. Reflectors placed in the crater enable laser range finders to chart growth inch by inch.

Top, helicopters served the brave scientists who studied Mount St. Helens in 1981, even making quick visits to the crater. Extreme heat, continued eruptions, and the presence of hydrochloric, sulfuric, and hydrofluoric acids made permanent instrumentation here impossible.

A lava dome forms within the mile-wide, fitful, steaming crater that was Mount St. Helens, opposite. By May 1981 the third of these domes to form was 350 feet high and 2,000 feet across.

uncorking a champagne bottle. Gases suddenly formed bubbles in the molten rock, causing the magma to expand explosively out the side of St. Helens. Screaming northward at 670 miles per hour, the spreading blast soon overtook the slower avalanche.

From his position on an exposed ridge, David Johnston could see the eruption racing toward his campsite. The 30-year-old scientist had just enough time to radio five words to his headquarters. "Vancouver, Vancouver. This is it," he yelled before the cloud shredded his trailer. When investigators later visited the site, they found a land stripped of all trees and even soil. In places, the blast had scoured the ridge down to bare rock.

The eruption of Mount St. Helens claimed 57 lives, making it by far the most deadly volcanic incident in U.S. history. But future eruptions along the Cascade Mountains could well dwarf the St. Helens disaster. A string of 20 other potentially active volcanoes runs along the Pacific Northwest coastline, from northern California all the way into southern British Columbia. One of these peaks, Mount Rainier, towers over the Seattle-Tacoma metropolitan area, only 20 miles away. In fact, 100,000 people live on the remnants of several tremendous mudflows that swept down the mountain hundreds and thousands of years ago.

Mount Rainier need not even erupt to extinguish the lives below. Glacial water on the mountain has combined with its own internal heat to gradually weaken much of Rainier's rock. In the past, whole sections of the mountain have collapsed in giant landslides. Volcanologists warn that pieces of the steep peak can break off during earthquakes or perhaps for no apparent reason. Huge rivers of mud and rock would barrel down river drainages toward cities built on the floodplains below. "A major volcanic eruption or debris flow could kill thousands of resi-

dents and cripple the economy of the Pacific Northwest," warns Smithsonian volcanologist Richard S. Fiske, who led a National Research Council study of Rainier's hazards in 1994.

Cascade volcanoes such as Rainier owe their existence to a plate tectonic smashup along the Pacific Northwest coastline. For nearly 40 million years, a patch of the Pacific seafloor has been ramming into North America and sliding beneath the continent. The oceanic plate sinks slowly into the hot mantle, gradually warming up until, at a depth of 60 miles, it starts to melt. Liquid and buoyant, the molten rock rises up through the crust to erupt along the Cascade Mountain Range.

Similar plate collisions occur around much of the Pacific Rim, spawning a vast chain of volcanoes known as the Ring of Fire, which reaches from Indonesia, up through Japan, Siberia, and Alaska and then down through the Americas.

In early 1993, six scientists and three tourists met untimely deaths while studying one dangerous peak in the Ring of Fire: a mountain called Galeras. Situated in the northern Andes, Galeras is the most active volcano in Colombia, threatening 400,000 people who live on its flanks. For that reason, a conference of experts met in the shadow of the volcano in January 1993 to discuss the risks it posed.

After the meeting, more than a dozen researchers hiked into the volcano's crater to collect samples of hot gases escaping from various vents in the rock. Andrew Macfarlane, a young geologist, remembers that the group split up to reach different vents, which were farther apart than he had anticipated.

Macfarlane's inexperience saved his life. If he had been more familiar with the sampling equipment he carried, he might have ventured into the crater to make the planned measurements. Instead, he decided to return to town to discuss the work with a more senior scientist. As

Some plant life was already emerging from Mount St. Helens' ash, above, in June 1980, only a month after the first explosion. A few frogs, beavers, and salamanders survived the eruption, but an estimated 2 million birds, fish, and other animals perished in the 232 square miles devastated by the blast.

Opposite, shattered 150-foot tree trunks looking like matchsticks litter the terrain below Mount St. Helens. Everything within 15 miles of the mountain's north face was flattened or buried by 670-mile-per-hour scorching ash clouds.

Mount St. Helens' ash blankets downtown Yakima, Washington, causing nightfall in the morning. Agricultural land was buried and the town's sewer system was overwhelmed.

Macfarlane and several others started to leave, they looked back toward their colleagues working on the crater floor and along the rim.

The crew hadn't descended more than 100 yards when they heard an explosion coming from inside the crater. A black cloud billowed above the volcano—rising from the very spot occupied by five researchers only seconds before. When a burning fragment clipped Macfarlane above the eye, he started running downhill, trying to dodge the large rocks dropping from the sky. Some were more than a yard across. The volcanic bombs shattered as they hit the ground, sending out a spray of red-hot shrapnel.

Tumbling and staggering down the mountain, Macfarlane passed a mortally wounded colleague covered in blood. A dead tourist lay on the ground, his clothes ignited by the burning rocks. The young scientist struggled on with bruised legs and one eye swollen shut until he collapsed on a steep uphill climb. Rescue workers finally reached him and three others who had escaped.

One of these survivors, Stanley Williams, suffered two broken legs and a fractured skull on Galeras. Even after his brush with death, Williams didn't lose his sense of humor. Weeks after the eruption, a doctor looked into his ear to investigate why Williams had lost hearing on that side. "The doctor was shocked to find—for the first time in his experience—a patient whose head actually had rocks in it," Williams joked. "Unfortunately, he didn't have enough sense to save the damn samples. I berated him repeatedly."

Williams and his colleagues will return to Galeras to renew their studies there. The dedicated scientists are drawn by the knowledge that Galeras had only hiccuped when their friends died in the crater. The mountain still smolders over hundreds of thousands of nearby residents and will someday unleash a much larger blast.

Compared to Galeras and other subduction volcanoes, the broad-shouldered mountains of Hawaii have a decidedly gentler eruptive style. The lavas emitted by Kilauea and other Hawaiian giants flow more smoothly than the sticky goop that clogs volcanoes along the Ring of Fire. These lava flows hardly ever kill people, although they often destroy homes and property.

The Hawaiian volcanoes don't have to erupt to pose a risk, however. The mountains rise so high above the seafloor that they cannot withstand gravity. Occasionally, part of a volcano will peel off in a mammoth landslide. Millions even trillions of tons of rock can plunge into the ocean, raising tsunamis of unimaginable proportions.

When one volcano sloughed off some of its exterior 105,000 years ago, a 1,070-foot-high wave pounded the shores of nearby islands, carrying coral up the sides of mountains. Such landslides occur infrequently, perhaps only once every 100,000 years, so it's unlikely the next one will strike anytime soon. But even a relatively mild version could prove devastating.

FIRE AND WATER

The word "eruption" brings to mind explosions full of sound and fury. Yet most of the world's volcanoes erupt in silence, without any witnesses. Hidden lava flows happen all the time in the deep ocean, miles beneath the waves. They

Left, an entrepreneur in Yakima, Washington, takes advantage of Mount St. Helens' fallout two days after the eruption, and almost 90 miles away.

Above, a bus driver struggles with the glassy volcanic particles in Kelso, Washington, after a small May 25 Mount St. Helens' eruption. Left, an estimated 600,000 tons of grit were removed from Yakima. Planes, trucks, cars, and trains were immobilized across the state of Washington for several days.

FOLLOWING THE FIRE

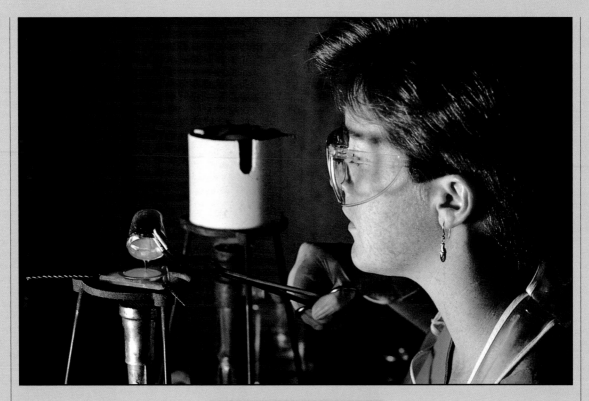

Smithsonian researcher Victoria Avery melts lava samples for analysis.

Right, Smithsonian and Japanese scientists work from a deep-diving Japanese submersible to recover rock and pumice samples, bottom.

When the world's scientists need information about volcanoes, they turn to the Smithsonian Institution in Washington, D.C. With 150 years of experience in volcanism, the Smithsonian runs a world center that relays reports of current eruptions and organizes records of past ones. Known as the Global Volcanism Program, and directed by Tom Simkin of the National Museum of Natural History, the center provides real-time information on every major eruption in the world. The extensive computer database that supports the program contains 10,000 years of information on volcanic activity.

The Smithsonian's Department of Mineral Sciences is itself a valuable resource for the world's small family of several hundred volcanologists. It is the location of the most compre-

hensive international collection of specimens from live volcanoes—about 6,500 items—and its archives contain rare volcanic maps, charts, seismic records, and field reports. The group also publishes a monthly publication, *Bulletin of the Global Volcanism Network*.

Smithsonian researchers conduct field research as well. An increasing amount of their work involves volcanic activity in the world's oceans, where most volcanoes can be found. Senior curator William G. Melson extracted the first important samples from the volcanically active mid-Atlantic Ridge. In 1993, research geologist Richard Fiske joined Japanese scientists in a deep-diving submersible to gather pumice from the western Pacific at a depth of 4,000 feet. Fiske says the exploration "pushes back the frontier of how undersea explosive volcanism differs from that on land." One use of the new knowledge might be insights into the origin and locations of valuable mineral deposits, including copper, zinc, gold, and lead. ■

occur along a 40,000-mile-long chain of volcanic mountains that winds around the globe like the seam on a baseball.

This mid-ocean ridge marks the border between spreading tectonic plates. As two plates separate, they open a wound through which molten rock can rise to the surface and harden. The young lava forms new ocean crust, which bonds to the edge of the receding plates.

In only a few places does the mid-ocean ridge rise above the waves and reveal how Earth's skin grows. The wind-swept island of Iceland is one such spot. Geologically speaking, Iceland is a divided nation. Half of the island sits on the North American plate, while the other half belongs to the Eurasian plate. Moving in opposite directions, the plates slowly tear Iceland in two, causing red-hot lava to erupt amid—and even underneath—its glaciers. This spreading process adds roughly 15 acres of smoking new real estate to the country every decade.

Over the centuries, the citizens of this living island have learned to cope with the ever-present threat of lava flows and other volcanic hazards. They have even fought back on occasion. In one of the greatest known tales of man versus nature, the country banded together to wage war on a volcano that sprouted on the outskirts of Vestmannaeyjar, a town on tiny Heimaey Island off the coast of Iceland.

On January 23, 1973, in the middle of the night, residents of Vestmannaeyjar woke up to a 500-foot-high curtain of lava erupting out of a mile-long gash in the ground. Soon, a cinder cone formed, throwing up ash and rocks that completely buried some nearby homes over the next few days. Then lava started flowing into town. The slow-moving streams inundated houses and threatened to block Heimaey's harbor, Iceland's most important fishing port.

Within six hours of the eruption's start, nearly all of Heimaey's 5,300 residents had evacuated to the mainland. But some of them soon returned to fight the eruption. For five months, they pumped seawater onto the advancing flows, cooling the 2,000-degree-Fahrenheit lava enough that it solidified. They eventually sprayed 6 million tons of water on the flows—roughly the amount that flows over Niagara Falls in 30 minutes.

Scientists cannot judge the success of the operation since no one knows how far the lava would have flowed if left to its own devices. But the town lost only a portion of its land and the harbor remained open—two facts that Heimaey residents count as a victory. They should also count themselves lucky. Had more lava poured out, no amount of spraying could have saved the town.

BLASTS FELT AROUND THE WORLD

Summer, 1816. North America shivers through record-setting cold. Snow falls in New England during June and July. In Europe, Lord Byron, Mary Shelley, and Percy Shelley spend a holiday in Switzerland, but the unseasonable rain and cold keep the three writers trapped indoors. Driven by the frightful weather, they engage in a contest to see who can write the best ghost story. Mary Shelley wins with a chilling—and enduring—tale entitled *Frankenstein*.

Historians refer to 1816 as the Year Without a Summer. The unusual weather North America and Europe experienced was an aftereffect of the largest eruption in the last millennium. In 1815, the Indonesian volcano Tambora let loose a blast more than 100 times larger than the one Mount St. Helens served up in 1980. The Tamboran explosion killed 10,000 people initially and 80,000 more through post-eruption disease and famine.

The 1815 eruption and others of its size shoot so much debris into the sky that all of humanity feels their power. In 1883, an explosion shattered

Ash blankets an Icelandic town, above. On the island of Heimaey in 1973, Icelanders helped to stop a lava flow from blocking their harbor by spraying it with seawater.

Opposite, ash and steam blast from the youthful island of Surtsey, Iceland, in August 1983. The volcano that formed Surtsey appeared above the waves in 1963. In 10 days it was an island, 2,952 feet by 2,132 feet.

the Indonesian island of Krakatau with such violence that it was heard nearly 3,000 miles away. The volcanic debris lofted into the stratosphere stained sunsets around the globe for seven years. In New York and Connecticut, the Sun's afterglow burned so vividly in the sky that people called out fire engines to extinguish what they thought were blazes.

In 1628 B.C., an eruption tore apart the Greek island of Thíra, leaving only the shell of a crater. With the island's destruction and the giant tsunamis triggered by the blast, distant observers may have thought that Thíra had disappeared into the sea. Some historians believe this ancient eruption actually spawned the myth of Atlantis.

Before the explosion, Minoan traders centered on nearby Crete dominated the Aegean Sea and had established a wealthy port on Thíra. Afterward, the influence of Minoan culture diminished and was eventually replaced by the emerging Mycenaean society on the Greek mainland. To some archaeologists, the timing seems more than coincidental. They think that the eruption on Thíra and the loss of this port could have helped topple Minoan power.

But even Krakatau, Tambora, and Thíra rank as minor pops when compared to the largest possible eruptions. Because they wrack the planet so infrequently, humanity has not witnessed one of these planet-wrenching events since before the dawn of civilization. But giant craters scattered around the globe provide silent testimony to past blasts.

Yellowstone National Park has a sunken scar measuring 45 miles long by 30 miles wide. Roughly 600,000 years ago, that corner of Wyoming hosted an eruption ten times bigger than Tambora's and 100 times bigger than the one that destroyed Krakatau.

The famous geysers of Yellowstone signal that this volcano remains hot and dangerous, with a supply of magma close to the surface. If the next

blast follows the pattern of its predecessors, it will cover the western half of the United States with a thick layer of ash.

When will Yellowstone roar into life again? It could happen next year, though the chances are exceedingly slim. Because the volcano waits hundreds of thousands of years between eruptions, the human species could disappear before Yellowstone next shows its strength.

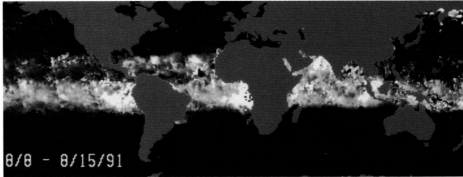

8/8 - 8/15/91

THE POWER TO PREDICT

Volcanic eruptions and earthquakes rock some part of the globe each week. Each year, they kill thousands. Human beings have lived in fear of such planetary spasms for countless generations, seeking protection from the gods on high. But surely with all the technological advances of the twentieth century, scientists will discover ways to predict death-dealing upheavals.

Volcanic experts have indeed made great strides in terms of forecasting eruptions. In the case of Mount St. Helens and again with Mount Pinatubo, researchers detected signs of danger months before the climactic blasts. Although they could not predict the actual day of the eruptions, volcanologists studying these mountains did provide enough warning to evacuate endangered communities.

At one time, some seismologists thought earthquake prediction was also within reach. In part, these hopes stemmed from the discovery of plate tectonics, which provided a general theory explaining why stresses accumulate in the crust.

Above, two months after the cataclysmic eruption of Mount Pinatubo on June 15, 1991, a cloud of volcanic dust had spread around the planet. Light-colored areas represent volcanic particles moving through the stratosphere.

Opposite, tumbling clouds of super-heated ash overtake a fleeing vehicle. The race for life occurred in 1991 when Pinatubo in the Philippines almost self-destructed on the island of Luzon. Military and Red Cross workers from around the world helped the Filipinos save lives and comfort displaced persons.

VOLCANO IN A CORNFIELD

Mexico's Paricutin in 1944, the year after its surprise eruption in a cornfield.

More than half-a-century has now passed since the weeks during early 1943 when residents of Paricutin in central Mexico first heard the ground speak. About 200 times a day, noises rumbled up from below the surface, and then the land trembled, filling the people with dread. They were about to witness what few have ever seen—the birth of a volcano.

Dionisio Pulido hadn't noticed anything unusual about his field until he visited it on February 20. At about 4 P.M., Pulido saw a long fissure cutting across the land. Moments later, the ground thundered and fine ash rose from the crack. With a loud whistling sound, the smoky cloud poured out faster and the stench of sulfur filled the air. Pine trees near the hole burst into flame. Pulido and his companions fled in fear of their lives.

During the night, villagers described tongues of flame reaching high into the sky as the infant volcano hurled boulders violently through the air. When Pulido returned the next morning, he found a small hill erupting rocks, ash, and lava in the middle of his field. The cone grew to a height of 160 feet in its first day. In a week, it stood 350 feet tall.

As ash rained over the landscape, some residents came to believe their plight was divine punishment for the destruction of a holy cross erected by priests to bring peace in a local dispute.

Four months after the eruptions started, villagers were forced to abandon Paricutin. Within a year, the blanket of pulverized volcanic rock had suffocated all plants within three to five miles of the growing cone, which people named after the town it had destroyed. By the time it went silent in 1952, Paricutin had reached a height of 1,390 feet.

Volcanologists from around the world made pilgrimages to Paricutin during the nine years that it was erupting, documenting in great detail the mountain's entire history, from birth until death. William Foshag, a Smithsonian mineralogist, visited Paricutin only a month after it sprouted and spent two and one-half years studying its growth. He and colleagues preserved the observations made by Dionisio Pulido and others who watched the birth of Paricutin.

While scientists found the volcano a gift of information, it was nothing less than a scourge for people uprooted by the eruptions. Roughly 4,500 cattle and 550 horses suffocated on fine ash during the early stage of the eruption. Although no humans died directly from the ash and lava, lightning sparked by Paricutin killed three people. The indirect toll ran even higher. At one resettlement center, 100 people died because of sickness, despondency, and the hostility of local residents.

Oddly, Paricutin continues to kill even four decades after it went quiet. Because the eruption erased traditional landmarks, it enhanced conflicts over property boundaries. In 1990, one man died during a dispute over land located near the volcano. ■

Enthusiasm also grew following a string of notable successes in which scientists accurately forecast tremors around the world.

The most famous of these feats occurred in China, a country that had launched an ambitious prediction effort in 1966 after a devastating earthquake killed 8,000 people in the city of Xingtai. The Chinese program marshaled the forces of thousands of seismic observers, who kept close tabs on areas of known earthquake danger. One of these hot spots was Liaoning Province in northeastern China, a place that showed numerous indications of impending activity.

In the winter of 1974, those warning signs grew more obvious. The level of underground water rose and fell. The ground surface tilted abnormally. Domestic animals behaved strangely, and snakes emerged into the frigid December air months out of season. Perhaps most ominous of all, a swarm of earthquakes jiggled the area.

In January 1975, concern increased when the unusual phenomena grew more pronounced and showed indications of spreading toward the cities of Haicheng and Yingkou. On February 1, a quake swarm started and gained intensity with each passing day. When the morning of February 4 brought a crescendo of 500 small to moderate quakes, the seismologists couldn't deny their fears any longer. They issued a prediction for a major earthquake to hit within the next day or two. Haicheng and Yingkou had to evacuate.

Hundreds of thousands of people complied, leaving their work and homes to wait outside in the bitter cold. Films were shown in parks and squares to encourage the evacuees to remain outdoors. Then at 7:36 P.M., when the citizens of Haicheng and Yingkou were thinking about returning to their warm homes, the quake came. Registering magnitude 7.3, the jolt tore through the poorly constructed buildings, leveling most of these two cities. Yet because of the evacua-

tion, only 300 died in the earthquake. The prediction had saved thousands, perhaps hundreds of thousands of lives.

That same year, Chinese seismologists successfully forecasted more earthquakes days to hours before they struck. In the United States, seismologists accurately foresaw a handful of small shocks in California and New York State, while Soviet scientists alerted people to a magnitude 7 jolt before it occurred in 1978.

But for every successful prediction, quake experts accumulated many more failures and false alarms. Most notable of all, the prediction techniques that averted a disaster at Haicheng did not work when a large earthquake struck the city of Tangshan a year later. That tragic shock on July 28, 1976, killed 250,000, according to reports at the time; some researchers believe the actual number lies closer to 750,000.

Over the years, U.S. scientists have suffered disappointments as well. While a string of major earthquakes has pounded western states in the last decade, researchers have not found any telltale signs heralding the arrival of these jolts. Like so many others before it, the Northridge quake in January 1994 came without warning.

Charlatans, fortune tellers, and even some scientists have tried to predict earthquakes using unconventional methods. In the late 1980s, a climatological consultant named Iben Browning triggered a quake scare in the central United States when he predicted that tidal forces would set off a strong tremor near New Madrid, Missouri, in early December 1990. Although Browning had no training in seismology, intense media coverage of the announcement caused many communities to take it seriously. The incident disrupted hundreds of thousands of lives and had an economic impact into the tens of millions of dollars from lost wages, emergency preparations, and other expenses. As for the earthquake, it never happened.

The U.S. government has so far sanctioned only one earthquake prediction—a medium—term forecast concerning the tiny town of Parkfield, California. Situated on the San Andreas Fault, Parkfield lies halfway between Los Angeles and San Francisco. In the last 150 years, this town has faced a remarkably regular series of strong quakes: tremors of magnitude 5.5 or 6 struck in 1857, 1881, 1901, 1922, 1934, and 1966. Except for the 1934 shock, the quakes came once every 22 years or so, almost as regular as clockwork.

On the basis of this record, seismologists with the U.S. Geological Survey predicted in 1985 that a magnitude 6 quake would shake Parkfield by the beginning of 1993. They wired the fault with millions of dollars' worth of equipment in order to catch the entire life cycle of the jolt. Researchers even planned to look for precursory signs hours to minutes before it actually arrived. If ever they had a shot at prediction, surely the clockwork quakes of Parkfield provided the best opportunity.

But as the January 1, 1993, deadline came and went, the San Andreas remained quiet. For U.S. seismologists, Parkfield was a disappointment that cut deep into their hopes for predicting earthquakes. Of all the spots in the world, this patch of the San Andreas produced the most regular quakes ever witnessed. But even Parkfield refused to follow a set pattern.

Scientists still believe that a jolt is due at Parkfield, and when it comes, the monitoring equipment set up on the fault should yield important clues. But researchers think they may have to discard the idea of reliable quakes. Instead, the San Andreas and other faults appear to behave chaotically.

Even though scientists can't predict the exact year or day a quake will strike, they can at least tell which areas of the world will most likely suffer seismic tremors in the next few decades. In

Left, Molokini, a submerged volcanic crater off Maui creates a pocket lagoon.

Above, trapped for eternity, a bus at Kalapana on the island of Hawaii failed to outrun a lava discharge. Stalwart villagers in the volcanic zone play cat-and-mouse with roiling rivers of molten stone.

Left, scientists of the United States Geological Survey take chemical specimens at Mount Baker, a volcano in the Cascades. This northwestern range, along with the states of Alaska and Hawaii, holds nearly all of the United States' active volcanoes.

Opposite, rivers of lava flow from Kilauea, located on the "Big Island" of Hawaii. During their surge to the sea, incandescent currents of rock bury or burn anything in their way.

Fire, water, and earth come together in nature's great laboratory, opposite. Here in Hawaii, lava courses to the sea either in open rivers or through tunnels of hardened lava.

theory, such long-term warnings can help cities plan for eventual disasters by giving them time to educate citizens, strengthen buildings, and train emergency personnel.

Several nations are also trying to develop quick response systems that will limit damage once an earthquake hits. This idea relies on the speed of radio waves, which travel 5,000 times faster than seismic vibrations. When sensors close to a fault first detect a strong quake, they can send out radio signals that arrive at critical facilities several seconds before the shaking. Although not enough to evacuate people, these warnings can provide time to alert police, mobilize fire trucks and ambulances, shut off gas mains, and perform other life-saving functions.

Yet despite the best efforts of scientists, the risks of natural disasters may actually be climbing. Population growth around the world has forced increasing numbers of people to settle in geologically unstable spots. In California, entire cities have grown astride the San Andreas and other dangerous faults. In the Pacific Northwest, towns have sprouted on the flanks of active volcanoes. The developing world faces even greater risks: witness the 22,000 deaths at Nevado del Ruiz in 1985.

The statistics for volcanic eruptions demonstrate all too dramatically humanity's increasing vulnerability. From 1600 to 1900, volcanoes killed an average of 315 people per year. Since the turn of the century, that mortality rate has increased to 845 per year.

Scientists can identify the hazards, but they cannot eliminate the risk as long as people live in geologically active regions. Only society can decide how to prepare for the inevitable convulsions of our living planet. History provides countless examples of what happens when the risks are ignored. "Civilization," observed writer Will Durant, "exists by geologic consent, subject to change without notice."

THE NATURE OF RISK

DENNIS FLANAGAN

HEN NATURE is on the rampage, human beings are at risk. They are at risk not only for death and injury but also for the loss of loved family members and friends, of their home, of their possessions, of their livelihood. They are also at risk for emotional stress and the loss of a sense of security.

The last is insidious and impossible to measure. It has to do with both the risks of the future and the risks of the past, since growing knowledge and understanding of past rampages affect expectations of future ones. For example, the July 1994 assault of Jupiter by Comet Shoemaker-Levy 9 probably gave many people a heightened appreciation for the possibility of such collisions with Earth. In addition, the perception of risk is strongly conditioned by experience. Someone who has never seen a tornado might think the chances of experiencing one are small, whereas someone who has seen one might think differently.

In order to function effectively and enjoy life, human beings need confidence. When a risk is perceived, correctly or otherwise, confidence is eroded. That being the case, the proper assessment of risk becomes an important human endeavor. Overestimating risk generates foolish fears; underestimating it, foolish unpreparedness.

When an earthquake was predicted at New Madrid, Missouri, on December 3, 1990, a church bulletin board, right, proclaimed the urgency of preparation. The earthquake never happened.

Below, floods, landslides, and mud avalanches plagued Californians in January 1982 killing 26, injuring 477, and damaging or destroying 6,535 homes. Mudslides are common in regions like the Santa Cruz Mountains, where fault movement grinds rock into a slippery substance.

Houses align precariously on the edge of California's Daly City, opposite, near the San Andreas Fault. Storms have quickly eroded the city's shores and slopes since the 1906 earthquake displaced land 13 feet and a 1957 tremor triggered avalanches.

Page 188: Slicing into Earth about six times deeper than the Grand Canyon, the Rio Grande Rift runs from Colorado into Texas along its namesake river. As plate movement and volcanic activity stretch the crust, they widen the rift, which is concealed from unsuspecting New Mexico residents by a filling of sediments and lava.

UNDERSTANDING NATURE'S RISKS

What precisely is meant by the word "risk"? In everyday usage, risk, hazard, danger, and peril can have different shades of meaning, but in the present connection risk means only one thing: the possibility that something bad is going to happen. The possibility is expressed in various ways, such as one chance in 100, 1 percent, or .01, each denoting the same probability. Each expression has its uses.

When it comes to the risks of rampaging nature, an important factor is uncertainty. Few risks are certain, that is, 100 percent. Moreover, most risks are dependent on time. For example, the risk that a major earthquake will strike Oakland, California, at some time in the future is for all practical purposes 100 percent, but the estimated risk that one will strike over the next 30 years is 28 percent.

The leading experts on risk are in the insurance industry, which is founded on making the most accurate risk assessments possible. But the insurance industry must also live with uncertainty. Life insurance is instructive. The risk of someone dying in the long run is 100 percent, but the risk of their dying at a given age is smaller. The latter risks have been calculated in great detail for actuarial tables, and insurance companies normally make a profit on life insurance.

It is harder to make a profit on other kinds of insurance because the risks are more uncertain.

The reason is what statisticians call the law of large numbers. Even though it cannot be predicted years in advance when someone will die, actuarial tables are based on so many millions of past life histories that the probability of someone dying at a certain age can be predicted with a high degree of accuracy. But with past earthquakes, say, the numbers are smaller and the predictions much less accurate.

Risks are dependent not only on time but also on place: it is well known that the risk of an earthquake in California is much greater than it is in Florida, and the risk of a hurricane-force windstorm in Florida is much greater than it is in California. Still, even though the risks of an earthquake in California and a hurricane in Florida are high, both are uncertain. One unfortunate result of these uncertainties is that insurance companies can be bankrupted by natural rampages that they were not able to predict well enough to have set the appropriate rates.

All the same, the art of reducing uncertainty has made progress. Consider the probabilities in time and space of six of the most frequent and most destructive rampages in the United States: hurricanes, tornadoes, floods, earthquakes, tsunamis, and volcanic eruptions.

RISKY RAMPAGES

Hurricanes are limited to the Atlantic and Gulf Coasts; Pacific hurricanes, or typhoons, occur only in the western Pacific. Hurricane risk is greatest in southern Florida and in western Florida along the Gulf Coast. It is measured by "occurrences of destruction" over a 50-year period. In those areas there have been more than 30 such hurricanes in the past 50 years; therefore the annual risk is at least 60 percent. For the other states along the Atlantic and Gulf Coasts the annual risk is between 10 and 30 percent.

Tornadoes can touch down in any state, but they are most frequent in certain areas of

Florida, Indiana, Kansas, Nebraska, Oklahoma, and Texas. There, the number of tornadoes per 100,000 square miles over a 28-year period has been seven to nine per year. Hence those areas are virtually certain to have one tornado a year: the annual risk is 100 percent.

Floods are the most frequent rampages of nature, but flood risk is hard to quantify because floods occur in so many different local circum-

stances. For floods that cover large areas, the Federal Emergency Management Agency (FEMA) takes a geologic approach: flood plains, areas where floods have deposited silt in the past, are the most likely places for floods to occur in the future. The states with the largest area of flood plain, and therefore those most likely to suffer such floods, are Arkansas, California, Florida, Louisiana, Mississippi, and Texas. The situation is different with floods on the seacoast. They are caused not by rain and runoff but by storm surges: water piled up by the force of strong winds. The risk of the most severe surges is correlated with the risk of hurricanes.

Opposite, the trans-Alaska pipeline snakes 800 miles from Prudhoe Bay to the ice-free port of Valdez. Although many Alaskans opposed its construction in the 1970s, the United States urgently needed the 2 million barrels of oil it would transport per day. Its zigzag construction allows the pipe to contract and expand with temperature changes and protects it from breaking during an earthquake.

Above, the curved shape of Arizona's Glen Canyon Dam helps it bear the stress of water pressure and 4.9 million cubic yards of concrete by transferring force to the side abutments and foundation, locking the dam against the canyon. During the 1983-84 floods, plywood flashboards and metal extensions offered temporary defense against waters rising above the dam. The Bureau of Reclamation may extend the height of the spillway gates or reduce the reservoir's water supply to provide more flood control space in the future.

Below, during an evening rush hour, nearly 3 million vehicles travel Los Angeles' 616-mile freeway system, whose elevated sections are necessary in California's terrain of hills and ravines.

Above, hydraulic vises squeeze test cylinders of concrete used in bridges and overpasses until they shatter. Concrete is strong when compressed but weak when stretched, so steel bars are used for strength and grout-filled steel jackets provide support.

Opposite, while most reinforced highways withstood the January 1994 earthquake, the Santa Monica Freeway buckled—it had been scheduled to be strengthened with steel in February.

Earthquakes can happen in any part of the country; the most violent series of earthquakes in U.S. history occurred in the central Mississippi Valley in 1811 and 1812. Earthquakes are most frequent, however, in areas of Alaska, California, Hawaii, and Nevada and in the area around Yellowstone National Park; those areas are designated "high hazard." Specific risk numbers are assigned to areas along well-studied geologic faults. For example, the risk that there will be one or more large earthquakes in the San Francisco area over a period of 30 years is 67 percent.

Tsunamis are high-speed ocean waves generated most often by undersea earthquakes. They can strike a coast with a series of devastating swells as much as 100 feet high. Since the preponderance of undersea earthquakes occurs in the tectonically active Pacific Basin, the U.S. areas at greatest risk are Hawaii and the West Coast (including Alaska). It is difficult to assign a specific risk for tsunamis because it is only in the past century that they have been recognized and recorded as such. In the past 100 years, however, at least 200 tsunamis—say two per year—have been recorded in the Pacific. Therefore the annual risk of there being a tsunami somewhere in the Pacific is virtually 100 percent. This, of course, does not mean that the risk of a tsunami hitting, say, Los Angeles, is 100 percent. All the same, there is a possibility that one will hit. The best way to deal with that possibility is prediction.

Volcanoes are found only in Hawaii and the western states (including Alaska). Eruptions are common in Hawaii and Alaska, but the only eruption since 1950 in the other 48 states was that of Mount St. Helens in 1980. Still, there are 20 other volcanoes in those states that have erupted in comparatively recent geologic times. Six of them, ranging from California north to Oregon and Washington, have erupted at least

Right, a time exposure captures the ranging beam of the two-color laser geodimeter used in experiments along the San Andreas Fault. As the laser hits 18 reflectors along the fault, changes in its travel time signal shifts in the ground.

Below, Rich Liechti, a U.S. Geological Survey technician, checks a creepmeter at Parkfield, California. The device can detect ground movements of only .0008 of an inch.

once every 200 years. Therefore the annual risk of their erupting is at least one in 200, or .5 percent.

At least two of these risks can be stated in a different way—the risk of dying. According to the Environmental Protection Agency (EPA), the risk of dying in a flood is one in 30,000 and the risk of dying in a tornado is one in 60,000. Many everyday risks are much greater. The risk of dying in an automobile accident is one in 100, of dying in a homicide one in 300, of dying in a fire one in 800. To be sure, the risk of dying of disease is greater still. Since cancer accounts for nearly a fourth of all deaths, the risk of dying from it is one in four. And since heart disease (exclusive of other cardiovascular diseases) accounts for a third of all deaths, the risk of dying from it is one in three. On the whole, the risks of dying from a rampage of nature are trivial by comparison with those that are all too familiar.

THE RISK OF GLOBAL WARMING

Many risks confronting human beings are created by human beings. Over the past 10,000 years, the species has had a substantial impact on the planet. It has cleared forests; replaced diverse plants over large areas with a few crop plants; accelerated soil erosion; created large urban areas; built dams, dikes, canals, roads, and tunnels; destroyed certain ecological systems and ecological niches; diminished the diversity of other species; and helped create dust bowls and deserts. Among the risks brought about by these activities are those of war, epidemic disease, famine, fires, dam breaks, air and water pollution, the addition of artificial carcinogens to natural ones, automobile, railroad, and airplane accidents, and industrial disasters. Because these risks are not attributable to rampages of nature (unless one considers the human species a slow rampage), they are largely beyond the scope of this discussion—largely, but not entirely.

Of all the risks created by human activities, the one that has attracted the most attention in recent years is the possibility that such activities are changing Earth's climate. The presumed cause is that the burning of fossil fuels (coal, gas, and oil) and the clearing of forests is increasing the concentration of carbon dioxide in Earth's atmosphere.

Carbon dioxide is only .03 percent of the atmosphere, but unlike the atmosphere's major constituents (nitrogen and oxygen) it is a greenhouse gas. A greenhouse gas is one that passes visible wavelengths but absorbs longer wavelengths such as infrared. When sunlight warms the earth's surface, its energy is reradiated as infrared; if there were no greenhouse gases, the infrared would simply go off into space. With greenhouse gases, it is absorbed and warms the atmosphere.

There can be no doubt that human activities have increased the amount of carbon dioxide in the atmosphere since the fires of the Industrial Revolution were lit. Since 1880, the amount has increased by perhaps 20 percent. Precise measurements starting in 1957 show that it continued to increase steadily—until the middle of 1991. Then, for reasons that are not understood, the rate of increase slowed. By the middle of 1993 it had resumed, and it seems likely that the general trend will continue. Moreover, at least until 1991, human activities had also increased the amounts of other greenhouse gases: methane, nitrous oxide, and carbon monoxide. The most abundant of all greenhouse gases is water vapor, and with a rise in temperature its concentration would also increase. What is the likelihood—the risk—that these increases, if they continue as expected, will make Earth warmer?

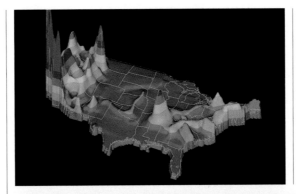

Left, using 350 years of historical data, a computer drew this map of earthquake-risk areas in the continental United States, flagging with red and purple the most seismically dangerous spots: the San Andreas Fault, the Cascade Range, Yellowstone, and the area surrounding New Madrid, Missouri.

Below, engineers use shake tables, which simulate seismic tremors of specific magnitudes, to test skyscraper models and other designs for safety and stability.

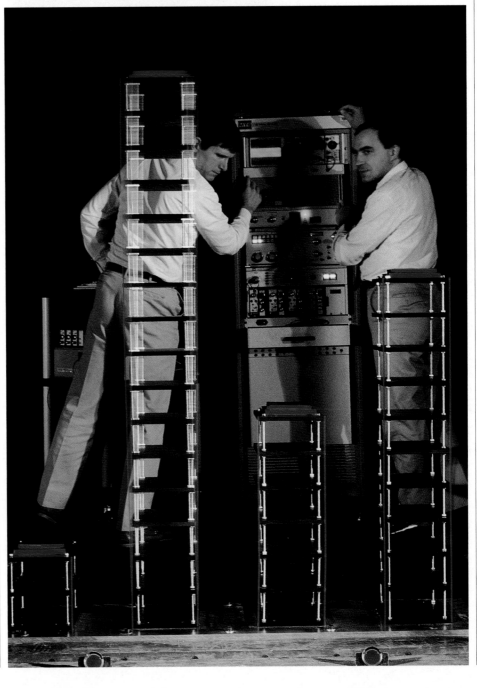

Nowadays, climatologists make their predictions by means of elaborate computer models, in which the major known factors influencing climate are mathematically integrated. Such models predict that a doubling of the concentration of carbon dioxide by the middle of the twenty-first century will cause a worldwide increase in temperatures of somewhere between 2.7 and 8.1 degrees Fahrenheit. In fact, temperature records from 1880 to 1980 show an increase in worldwide temperatures of .72 degree Fahrenheit, equivalent to .0072 degree per year. This last figure, however, does not rise above the noise level of the annual fluctuation in temperature: plus or minus .36 degree. As a result, global warming has not been strongly confirmed so far.

The main problem is that the concentration of carbon dioxide is only one of many variable factors that influence Earth's climate. Among the others are (1) small changes in the brightness of the Sun, (2) cyclic shifts in Earth's orbit and the tilt of its axis that slightly increase or decrease the amount of solar energy received by the Northern Hemisphere in summer, (3) changes in the position of land masses through continental drift that alter temperature-distributing patterns of oceanic circulation, and (4) periods of mountain building and continental uplift that alter patterns of atmospheric circulation.

To be sure, all of these latter factors operate over thousands and millions of years, not one century. Nevertheless, one or all of them may well account for such profound changes in climate as the ice ages. There is a widespread impression that the last Ice Age has long since ended, but in fact it is still in progress; there is plenty of ice on the planet. The present climate may even be a brief warm period before the next major advance of the glaciers.

Other complications enter in. For example, as can be seen in those lovely photographs of

Left, giant piers link 60-foot-high movable gates that form the Thames barrier, eight miles downstream from London, England, at Woolwich. During a surge tide or flood of the Thames River, the gates—each built to withstand more than 9,000 tons of water—are swung into place to prevent billions of dollars in property damage.

Earth from space, clouds are white, so they reflect away a substantial amount of the sunlight received by Earth. Clouds, of course, are condensed water vapor, and water vapor is generated by the warming of the oceans and other waters. This points to a possible negative-feedback mechanism: when Earth gets warmer, more water is evaporated, more clouds form, more sunlight is reflected and Earth gets cooler. No one can say, however, whether such feedback mechanisms are sufficient to maintain the temperature of Earth in a steady state if the concentration of carbon dioxide is substantially increased.

Above, torrential rains deluged Khartoum, the capital of Sudan, on August 4 and 5, 1988, causing the city's worst floods of this century. In two days, eight inches of rain fell, seven inches above the previous year's total. The floodwaters, from the nearby Blue and White Niles, left more than 1.5 million residents homeless.

Opposite, fishermen crowd an islet in the Bohol Strait near Cebu, Philippines, in 1985. Many of the country's islands experience severe erosion and overpopulation, as well as the destructive effects of volcanoes and tsunamis.

Many leading atmospheric scientists—by no means all—believe that the threat from added carbon dioxide is a grave one. They point to the serious effects that such warming might have for the human population: more intense storms, heavier rainfall, and a melting of ice sheets that would cause a rise in the sea level and drown the great coastal cities and low-lying areas such as the Netherlands. It is granted, however, that the effects would not be all bad: an increase in the concentration of carbon dioxide would enhance the growth of plants, which do, after all, make themselves out of carbon dioxide.

Nevertheless, serious proposals are before the governments of the world to reduce the amount of carbon dioxide pumped into the atmosphere by human activities. Such proposals call for limiting the burning of fossil fuels and the clearing of forests. That would mean, among other things, more reliance on other sources of energy. One is nuclear power, which most people today, rightly or wrongly, do not want. Another is solar power, which costs much more than most people realize, largely because it must somehow be stored in order to fill the demand when the Sun is not shining. The cost of any massive change in energy sources would clearly be hardest on poor countries, if indeed they could afford it at all.

But what is the risk that more carbon dioxide will make the world warmer? There is no question that the concentration of carbon dioxide in the atmosphere has increased and is continuing to do so, or that carbon dioxide is capable of warming the atmosphere. The heat of carbon-dioxide-rich Venus and the chill of carbon-dioxide-poor Mars are evidence enough. Whether or not the predicted increase in carbon dioxide will actually cause a rise in temperatures on Earth, however, is not definitely known. The risk is uncertain, and a plausible number cannot be assigned to it.

Citizens and their governments are left with a range of choices between doing something about the risk and doing nothing. Doing something that would substantially reduce the increase of carbon dioxide in the atmosphere would be immensely costly, but doing nothing might in the long run be even more so. There are possible compromises. One is a no-regrets policy, in which steps that make sense for economic and environmental reasons besides global warming would be taken first. Then, as the risks of warming became less uncertain, other steps could be added. An example of a first step would be a more aggressive effort to limit the clearing of the tropical rain forests.

Given the magnitude of the potential effects and the uncertainty of the risk, it seems certain that the issues they raise will be with us for a long time to come.

THE MANAGEMENT OF RISK

In the United States, risk is managed in divers ways by federal and state executive, legislative, and judicial bodies; by rules, regulations, and laws; by the insurance industry; by local communities, and by citizens acting on their own behalf. Three basic questions of risk management are: What is the risk? What can be done to diminish it? If a risk is realized, what can be done to reduce the effects?

For the assessment of risk, citizens are dependent on the opinion of experts: scientists, engineers, epidemiologists, and others who spend their professional lives assessing one risk or another. Many citizens, however, are skeptical of expert opinion and on occasion take issue with it. In a democratic system, that is their right, but there are times when the skepticism of a few citizens may require a community expenditure that is out of scale with any possible benefit. Moreover, there are times when concerned citizens demand that a perceived risk be more

intensively examined by experts. Both call for judgments on cost-effectiveness and the budgeting of resources.

Given the general acceptance of a risk assessment made by an expert, what can be done on the basis of that assessment to limit the effects of a rampage of nature? There are two main approaches: short-range prediction and long-range preparation. In the short-range prediction of some rampages (as distinct from long-range predictions based on probabilities) much progress has been made.

The observation of burgeoning hurricanes by weather satellites and other means has made it possible to predict some days in advance that a storm will arrive in a given area. This allows time for preparation, to batten down the hatches to the extent possible and, if it seems advisable, to evacuate. Tornado watches can give people in tornado-prone areas some warning—not enough time for them to prevent damage, but at least enough for them to be ready to seek shelter on short notice.

Flood warnings are a mixed bag. The slow rise of a large river can give ample warning, but a flash flood is the result of a largely unpredictable local rainfall. All the same, one flood warning system has saved tens of thousands of lives. The seacoast storm surges that flood as much as a quarter of Bangladesh have drowned as many as 300,000 people. Recently, storm-surge warnings have allowed time for evacuation and have made the loss of life almost negligible by comparison.

Earthquakes are the great dream of short-range prediction. There have been many promising leads but no real ability to predict an earthquake a few hours or days ahead of time. In February 1975, the Earthquake Research Branch of the province of Liaoning in northeastern China—having noted signs such as the spouting of wells, the strange behavior of animals, and, most important, a swarm of small earthquakes— predicted that a

Above, Houston, Texas, workers begin the arduous process of repair after Hurricane Alicia in August 1983. High winds, floods, and fires during the storm caused an estimated $1.5 billion in damage. Alicia generated 115-mile-per-hour winds and shattered windows, opposite, in the InterFirst and Allied Bank buildings.

major quake was about to strike the large city of Haicheng. On February 4, the provincial government ordered the city evacuated. Only nine hours later Haicheng was hit by an earthquake of magnitude 7.3; the evacuation had prevented a catastrophic loss of life. In spite of this notable success there was no early warning to the Chinese city of Tangshan on July 28, 1976, and an earthquake measuring 7.8 killed at least 250,000 people, perhaps many thousands more. The portents of Haicheng are simply not universal.

Since tsunamis are caused mostly by earthquakes, predicting them is no easier. Progress has been made, however, with warning of a tsunami that is already on its way. A tsunami can travel at hundreds of miles per hour in the open ocean, and it can also travel for thousands of miles; therefore, shorelines far enough from the source can be warned that one is coming. Unfortunately, it is not possible to predict how high the waves will be, so evacuation may turn out to be needless.

An internationally sponsored Pacific Tsunami Warning Center has been established in Hawaii. It operates by monitoring undersea earthquakes, and locating their epicenter, and determining their intensity. Then it passes the information along to local authorities on the shorelines that may be hit.

Volcanic eruptions are usually preceded by tiny earthquakes and belches of steam and gas, but these symptoms can go on for months or years and come to nothing. What is needed is a means of predicting an eruption shortly before it lets go. Geologist Stanley Williams and his colleagues found a promising method—the hard way. As seven of them were conducting observations on the volcano Galeras in Colombia in January 1993, the volcano exploded, killing six and severely injuring Williams. Before this disaster they had observed not only tiny earthquakes but also a decrease in the volcano's emission of sulfur dioxide. This suggested that the gas was being bottled up and pressure inside the volcano was rising. Other colleagues of Williams found the same pattern before a larger eruption in March 1993. The two symptoms occurring together may serve to predict other eruptions.

On the whole, long-range preparation is a better bet than short-range prediction. The best case is presented by earthquakes. Knowledge of how earthquakes cause damage and casualties steadily advances. So does the design of earthquake-resistant structures. The building codes of cities that are at risk of earthquakes increasingly take cognizance of these lessons. It is too much to expect an earthquake-proof city anytime soon, but in the long run, investment in earthquake-resistant buildings and other structures is bound to be profitable.

Investment in preparedness is also bound to be profitable, not only for earthquakes, but also for other natural disasters. The dissemination of information about the risk and how to deal with its realization—education across the board, starting in kindergarten—is perhaps the measure most likely to be productive. Emergency services and drills are valuable. To reduce the impact of disasters, the Federal Emergency Management Agency (FEMA) recommends that everyone threatened by one be prepared to be self-sufficient for at least 72 hours.

THE SHARING OF RISK

The key word in dealing with the risks of natural disasters is sharing. The risks are shared in two senses: civic responsibility for preparedness and recovery, and the cost of the disaster after it has happened. Much of the cost is borne by the insurance industry out of funds accumulated through the payment of premiums. Insurance companies, however, reinsure themselves, which means that if they lose money on insurance, the loss is covered by the reinsurance companies and may have to be shared by those who have invested in them.

Left, exposed fire hydrant piping and houses once stood a safe distance from the Atlantic. Here on Westhampton Beach, one of the Long Island, New York, barrier islands, erosion rates can reach 10 feet per year.

Below, a beach house lies toppled after a December 1992 northeaster hit Fire Island, another of the thin barrier islands off Long Island.

Opposite, homeowners watch helplessly as the Pacific smashes against the supports of their Malibu, California, beach house during a storm in 1983.

Left, coffins float beneath old cypress trees in Albany, Georgia, in July 1994 during several weeks of flooding that left 30 people dead. Hundreds of coffins were unearthed when the Flint River inundated cemeteries with shallow gravesites.

Losses are also shared by the public sector—the taxpayer. In some situations where insurance is essential but insurance companies are unwilling to take a high risk, the federal government underwrites the insurance. Such insurance is written by private companies, but the Federal Insurance Administration guarantees to compensate them for losses. An example is the federal flood-insurance program. To the public sharing of losses must be added federal disaster relief.

In recent years this system of cost sharing has been hit by a series of earthquakes—both literal and figurative. Estimated losses from the Carolinas' Hurricane Hugo in 1989 were $4.2 billion—the first to go over $1 billion. They were succeeded by losses of, among others, $16 billion from Florida's Hurricane Andrew in 1992 and $15 billion from California's Northridge earthquake in 1994. No one had predicted such gargantuan losses. The problem is whether the cost-sharing system, private and public, can withstand more of them without collapsing.

How is it that the losses from rampages of nature have become so much larger? The main answer is urbanization. When people and their multifarious works are concentrated in one area, a natural disaster will do more damage than it would in a less heavily populated area. Recognition of this fact is giving rise to much soul-searching among those who have the responsibility of making the cost sharing work.

Risk assessment is also a shared responsibility. When citizens urge their government to take action on a risk, they need to bear in mind that the cost is ultimately borne by themselves as taxpayers. If the risk should be a marginal one, spending public money on such action usually means spending less on other things that may not have attracted as much attention but may be more essential. Even if the action is passed along to private companies, as it is when manufacturers are required to make a change in a

More than a million volts charge a simulated lightning bolt, above. It strikes a scale model of a Boeing 777 airliner at Lightning Technologies in Pittsfield, Massachusetts. Although commercial aircraft are often hit by lightning, metal surfaces and devices that shield electronic equipment prevent severe damage.

Opposite, Breakers Waterpark patrons in Tucson, Arizona, seem oblivious to lightning. Care is taken, though, to clear the pool before storms come closer. Nearly 100 Americans die from lightning every year, and residents of central Florida see the most flashes.

product because of a marginal risk, the cost is borne by the buyer in higher prices. In the end, then, risk is best shared by individual citizens acting rationally in their own interest.

COST-EFFECTIVE PUBLIC EDUCATION

For citizens to act rationally requires that they be well-informed. Much has been said about the need for citizens to be better educated in science and technology. A powerful example is presented by a case of risk assessment: the 15-year effort to determine whether or not human health is jeopardized by electromagnetic fields. Although the alleged hazard is one created not by rampaging nature but by human activities, it has thrown a bright light on problems of risk management in both realms.

As the word indicates, an electromagnetic field has two components: electric and magnetic. Actually, the effects of external electric fields on human health are not at issue; they do not penetrate into the body. External magnetic fields, however, do penetrate the body. They are omnipresent in the modern human environment, generated mostly by electric power lines.

In 1979 Nancy Wertheimer, a free-lance epidemiologist, and Ed Leeper, a physicist, published a paper in the *American Journal of Epidemiology* reporting a statistical association between childhood leukemia and chronic exposure to low-level electromagnetic fields generated by low- and medium-voltage power lines. The paper attracted much attention, and later studies by other epidemiologists seemed to confirm the association. The finding was made even more widely known by a series of articles in *The New Yorker* by journalist Paul Brodeur.

Childhood leukemia is a rare disease. A 1992 Swedish study found a doubling of the normal incidence of the disease among 127,383 children who had lived within 300 meters of high-voltage transmission lines over a period of 25 years. The actual number of cases, however, was only 39, so a doubling would have been an excess of 20 cases, less than one additional case per year. This can scarcely be taken as proof of an association between high-voltage transmission lines and childhood leukemia. Furthermore, a study of the causes of 4,000 deaths among 223,000 electric-utility workers in France and Canada over a period of 20 years shows no excess deaths from leukemia, brain cancer, or prostate cancer.

Nevertheless, the possible association continues to be investigated, even by scientists skeptical of it. The cost of such research, borne mostly by public agencies and the electric-power industry, is estimated to have reached nearly $1 billion. Has this trip, so to speak, been necessary?

Magnetic fields are omnipresent not only in the human environment, but also in the natural environment. Earth has its own magnetic field, generated by ponderous flows deep in the planet's electrically conducting interior. The unit of measurement for the strength of a magnetic field is the gauss, and Earth's field varies from 300 milligauss (.3 gauss) at the equator to 700 milligauss (.7 gauss) at the poles. A representative value for the continental United States is 450 milligauss.

How does this natural field compare to the artificial fields generated by power lines? The magnetic fields to which people are subjected in the home typically have a strength of half a milligauss—perhaps 1 percent of the natural field. In the worst case anyone can think of, including ground zero under a 750,000-volt power line, the strength of the artificial field is less than 10 percent of that of the natural field. In other words, the artificial fields are drowned out by the natural one.

What some have speculated, however, is that biological effects could be the result not of the strength of the artificial fields but of the fact that they oscillate: the magnetic field of a 60-cycle

power line changes its polarity 120 times a second. Such oscillating fields do generate electric fields inside the body, but since the artificial fields are tiny, the electric fields they generate are also tiny. They are drowned out by the many natural electric fields already present in the body. There is an electric charge across the outer membrane of every living cell, and the impulse transmitted by a nerve fiber is electrochemical.

In order for a magnetic field to have any biological effect, it has to produce changes in living tissue. In fact, magnetic fields can produce such changes, but not at the frequencies of interest here. For example, every molecule of living tissue is held together by electromagnetic forces. A change such as a cancer-causing mutation requires that such molecules be ionized. Such disruption would call for a field with a frequency of 6 trillion cycles.

It would seem highly unlikely, to say the least, that electromagnetic fields are a threat to human health. Nevertheless, the body politic continues to respond as though it were a distinct possibility. Legislatures are currently considering immensely costly measures to protect the public against electromagnetic fields, schools have been moved away from power lines, lawsuits have been brought against power companies and electrical-equipment makers. People are having difficulty selling property near power lines. Already the overall cost, mostly from the loss of real estate values, has been estimated at $54 billion.

It has had the inexorability of Greek tragedy. Virtually every meeting held on the subject ends with a call for further costly research. Appointed public and private officials seem unwilling to dismiss the possibility of a threat lest they appear to have closed minds. Elected officials are concerned that failing to support protective measures will cost them votes. In other words, few decision-makers seem inclined to take any personal risk.

Above, Siberian women sunbathe during their very brief summer on the Ob River near Novosibirsk. Siberia's cities are among the former Soviet Union's most polluted, with the Ob itself awash in oil, pesticides, heavy metals, and sewage.

Los Angeles' infamous smog, top, as seen in this 1991 photograph of Hollywood, is a witch's brew of nitrogen oxide, sulfur dioxide, and hydrocarbons. These react with sunlight to produce a corrosive haze.

Opposite, oil wells blaze in Kuwait after the 1991 Persian Gulf war. Smoke clouds from more than 500 fires billowed for months.

The great question is: Could all this have happened if the public had been better informed about science and technology and statistics? If it had known, even in a general way, what is really at issue, would it not have dismissed the threat at the beginning? Would its national and local representatives not have done the same?

The episode demonstrates that too much concern with risks may not be a good thing. Life is inherently risky. Perhaps the riskiest course of action for an individual or a community would be to try to avoid all conceivable risk; the result would be paralysis.

THE RISK OF COSMIC COLLISION

The worst rampage of nature anyone can imagine is one that fortunately has not happened since human beings came into existence. It would be for a good-sized asteroid or comet to crash into Earth. If the object were, say, the size of Manhattan, and there are many asteroids and comets that are larger, it could extinguish the human species and most other living species as well. It is extremely unlikely that this will happen in the next 100 or 1,000 years, but the interesting thing is that it is by no means totally unlikely. The possibility is notably brought to mind by the recent bombardment of the planet Jupiter by the fragments of Comet Shoemaker-Levy 9. What, then, is the risk of something similar happening to our own planet?

Earth and all the other bodies in the Solar System were created 4.6 billion years ago out of a cloud of gas and dust. They were built by myriad collisions, ranging from collisions between molecules and dust grains to collisions between objects the size of a planet. The Moon is covered with craters made by bodies that have bashed into it. Most of these collisions took place before 3.8 billion years ago; the Moon is a fossil of that early time in the life of the Solar

System. Earth itself would look more like the Moon if its craters had not been erased by the action of its windy and watery atmosphere and the recycling of its surface by plate tectonics. Even so, there are at least 140 identifiable impact craters on Earth that were made recently enough to have survived.

When we contemplate the Solar System, with its planets and moons wheeling in their apparently changeless orbits, it seems almost crystalline in its purity. The fact is that the Solar System is full of junk. Some of it is debris left over from the formation of the system, some of it is asteroids that appear to be relics of a planet that never quite shaped up between the orbits of Mars and Jupiter, some of it is rocks and chunks of iron resulting from the asteroids banging into one another, and some of it is comets.

Earth is subjected to a steady rain of this celestial junk. Most of it is small stuff that burns up high in the atmosphere and streaks across the sky as meteors. Some of it is substantial objects that explode when they are heated by plunging into the atmosphere and never reach the Earth's surface. A fair amount of it, however, does reach the surface every once in a while with dramatic effect. Some 50,000 years ago, a fragment of a shattered asteroid, a chunk of iron estimated to have been 150 feet across, smashed into the ground near what is now the town of Winslow, Arizona. It exploded with the force of a 30-megaton bomb and excavated a crater eight-tenths of a mile across and more than 750 feet deep. Today Meteor Crater is one of the favorite tourist attractions of the American West.

How did a fragment of an asteroid happen to be in these parts, anyway? The overwhelming majority of such fragments travel between the orbits of Mars and Jupiter, where they were created by collisions between larger bodies. The fact is that the orbits of bodies in the Solar System are not inevitably stable and unchanging;

A tiny insect immigrant, above, the Mediterranean fruit fly (*Ceratitis capitata*) was first detected in the Los Angeles Basin of California in 1975. The fly has put the state's $2 billion per year agricultural harvest at risk, and inspectors, left, are constantly searching for infestation.

Opposite, dead cattle strew the landscape near Cameroon's Lake Nyos, which fills a volcanic crater. On August 21, 1986, the crater suddenly belched immense volumes of carbon dioxide. Sweeping down valleys, the gas asphyxiated 1,700 people and almost all other animal life.

the motions of such bodies can become chaotic and unpredictable, particularly if they are small bodies in the vicinity of mighty Jupiter. As a result, the Solar System is full of good-sized wanderers, some of whose altered orbits cross Earth's orbit. This is not to say that they are on a collision course with Earth but that they have the potential to collide with it.

Some of the wanderers are not fragments of asteroids, but comets. A comet is a big chunk of dirty ice, or icy dirt, that coalesced out of snowy particles at a distance far beyond the orbit of the outermost planet; such particles may well be the outer fringe of the cloud of gas and dust that gave rise to the Solar System in the first place. From time to time one of these dirty icebergs plunges toward the Sun and into the realm of the planets, where it is heated by sunlight and forms the luminous tail that excites wonder on the Earth. Repeated heating on later passes eventually drives off the volatile material in the comet so that it loses its tail; the comet is dead, but its corpse remains in orbit around the Sun.

As wanderers go, the 150-foot object that dug Meteor Crater was not particularly big. Among the objects whose orbits have been discovered to cross the orbit of Earth is one labeled 1627 Ivar, which is five miles across. What would happen if such an object were to hit Earth? There is, in fact, good reason to believe that an object of comparable size did hit Earth quite late in the 4.6 billion years of geologic history, with spectacular results.

Everyone's favorite mystery about the evolution of life on Earth is why the dinosaurs died out, which they did some 65 million years ago. In fact, at that time something happened that extinguished half the living species on Earth, including species as small and ubiquitous as marine plankton. A leading candidate for the cause of this carnage is the impact of a giant meteoroid that would have disrupted the ecolog-

Most meteorites are the size of sand grains, but Ahnighito, above, the 34-ton, iron specimen from Cape York, Greenland, survived its fiery ride through the atmosphere. Now at New York's American Museum of Natural History, this meteorite is the second largest known.

Streaking across Jackson Lake, Wyoming, opposite, a meteor of about 1,000 tons was captured on film in this August 1972 photograph. Thousands of meteoroids amounting to 50 tons of stone and metal hit Earth's atmosphere every day.

The first photographs of the Tunguska destruction, above, were not taken until about 20 years after the 1908 event.

The mysterious celestial explosion of June 30, 1908 that devastated more than 1,300 square miles of eastern Siberia's remote Tunguska region produced a blinding light followed by heat and shock waves felt for hundreds of miles. Witnesses said that a fireball with a burning tail perhaps 500 miles long incinerated everything beneath ground zero. One of the area's nomadic residents reported that his shirt was set ablaze. Others told of a force that picked them up, tossed them about, and knocked them unconscious. The blast leveled pine forests and destroyed herds of reindeer.

The first known outside visitor to glimpse the epicenter of destruction was stunned by the explosion's magnitude. "This is where the thunder and lightning fell down," he said.

Tunguska's mysteries are now being revealed thanks to recent scientific knowledge and access made possible by the region's political changes. Among the tools being used to study the airburst are spacecraft observations, supercomputers, precision measurements for orbital navigation as well as mass and energy transfer, and an understanding of the physical composition of bolides—meteorites and comets that collide with planetary bodies, including Earth.

Calculations from NASA suggest that the Tunguska event happened when a stony meteoroid exploded and vaporized perhaps 30,000 above the Tunguska River with its surrounding swamp and forest. The body itself, according to Christopher Chyba of the Goddard Space Flight Center,

was about 40 yards in diameter. No crater has been found, which would probably have been the case if the object had been a stronger iron specimen. In contrast, the meteoroid which struck 65 million years ago near what today is Mexico's Yucatán Peninsula, opposite page lower right, is estimated to have been about six miles across and dug a crater 100 miles or more in diameter.

While few people were killed in the sparsely populated Tunguska region of Siberia east of the Ural Mountains, in a more populous setting such a cataclysm would undoubtedly take many lives. Cosmic impacts are extraordinarily rare, occuring perhaps once every 2,000 to 12,000 years. But Tunguska is the most energetic shooting star reported since antiquity, and reminds us what we might expect in the future. ■

ical system to such an extent that highly special-ized organisms such as dinosaurs would not have been able to adapt to the change. The evidence for this hypothesis has been getting stronger.

For one thing, a crater has been found that is not only the right age but also the right size to have been made by an impact that could have had such an effect. Buried under sediments on the coast of the Yucatán Peninsula of southern Mexico, the crater is at least 110 miles in diameter and was blasted out by an explosion with a force of at least 100 million megatons. The results must have been truly catastrophic, not only in that part of the world but also in the rest of it.

The crater has been named Chicxulub. There is much evidence that the main effect of the impact that excavated it was not the immediate explosion but the injection into the stratosphere of huge quantities of dust. Such dust would have taken years to settle out, during which time it would have blocked much of the sunlight reach-ing Earth's surface. The lovely blue Earth revealed in photographs made from space would have been a dirty gray, and all plants, which rely on sunlight to build themselves by photosynthe-sis, would have been hit hard. The same would have been true of all animals, which depend ulti-mately on plants for food.

Part of the evidence for these catastrophic effects is a curious passage in the climate of the last century. Weather records in the United States and Europe for the year 1816 show that its sum-mer was weirdly cold. For example, there were freezing conditions in New England as late as July. Harvests suffered greatly. Much later, con-ditions in this Year Without a Summer were cor-related with a major eruption in the preceding year of the volcano Tambora on the Indonesian island of Sumbawa, which threw up such enor-mous quantities of dust and aerosols such as droplets of sulfuric acid that the sky over the entire planet was dimmed.

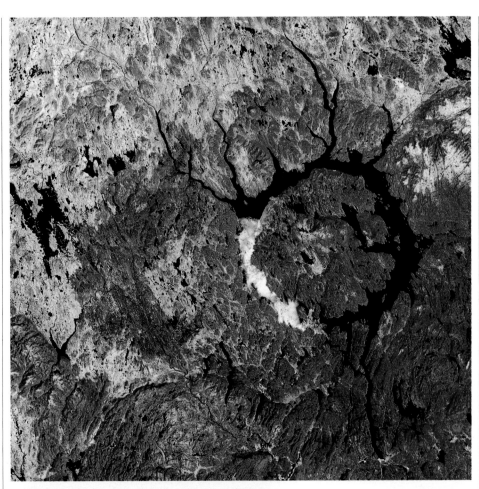

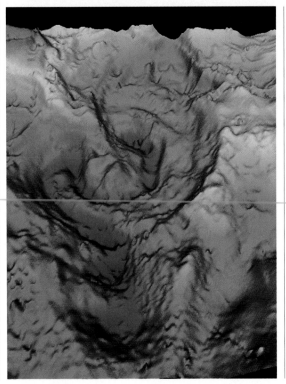

Top, the prehistoric Manicouagan crater in Quebec, Canada, is 41 miles across and may be the artifact of a massive meteoric blast.

Left, a computer-generated image of the Chicxulub crater in Mexico (see map above) which may be one of the largest meteor impacts of all time. Now buried, Chicxulub could be 186 miles across, and is strongly suspected of leading to the demise of half the species then alive—including dinosaurs.

Right, backlighting adds fire to the olivine inclusions in this polished section of the Imilac pallasite a distinctive iron meteorite found in Antofagusta, Chile, and held by collector Robert Haag.

Center, Wethersfield, Connecticut, assistant fire chief John McAuliffe examines a hole made by a six-pound meteorite in November 1982. This was the second home damaged by space debris in Wethersfield within a year.

Mrs. Hewlett Hodges, of Sylacauga, Alabama, bottom, was struck and bruised by a meteorite in her home in 1954.

Opposite, 50,000-year-old Meteor Crater in Arizona is approximately one mile across and was probably 750 feet deep originally. A 300,000-ton meteorite created this circular scar, technically known as an astrobleme.

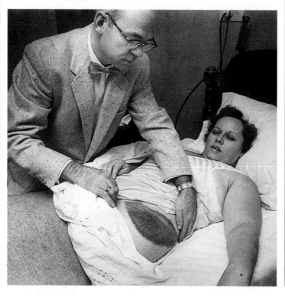

The effects of a Chicxulub-sized impact would of course be far worse. What is the probability that such a thing will happen again? In fact, it is 100 percent, given enough time; the objects are out there, and one big impact every 65 million years or so is not all that many in the sweep of Earth's history. Moreover, smaller impacts are proportionately more probable, and they, too, could have devastating effects, even if they did not extinguish the human species. The wild card in this cosmic game is that same species. If it was seriously threatened by an impending impact, could it perhaps do something to avert it?

The best answer has been given by astronomers Clark R. Chapman and David Morrison. They have taken extraordinary pains to assess the probability of catastrophic impacts on Earth and to consider what might be done to avert them. Their argument and their conclusions are presented in a scientific paper, already a classic, appearing in the journal *Nature* for January 6, 1994.

Chapman and Morrison conclude that the risk that an asteroid or comet a mile in diameter will collide with Earth over the next century, killing a large fraction of the human population, is one in 10,000. That may seem like a small risk, but Chapman and Morrison point out that it is comparable to risks we are quite used to thinking about. The risk of dying in an airplane crash is smaller: one in 20,000. This immediately suggests that since we take steps to reduce the number of airplane-crash fatalities, perhaps we should do the same for an asteroid or comet impact.

Curiously, asteroids and comets present somewhat different problems. Once an asteroid has been detected and its orbit determined, one can keep tabs on it and have several years' warning that it is headed this way. The same is true for short-period comets, which have been

Artist Don Davis depicts nature's greatest rampage: a large planetary body colliding with Earth. Everything within hundreds of miles is vaporized in seconds, and a chain reaction of volcanoes, earthquakes, and tsunamis begins. Wildfires cover the planet, as millions of tons of crushed rock and steam enter the stratosphere. Acid rain could fall for years, and global darkness could bring years of cold and the death of most living organisms.

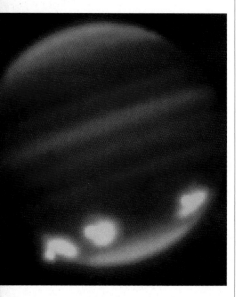

Above, an infrared image of Jupiter shows brightly glowing impact sites, each larger than Earth, caused by fragments of Comet Shoemaker-Levy 9. From July 16 to July 22, 1994, the world watched as at least 21 pieces of the comet's original nucleus penetrated the planet's gas atmosphere. The chunks ranged in size from 1,000 yards to two miles across, and were created when Jupiter's gravity broke the comet apart in 1992. They struck at a speed of 134,000 miles per hour with a combined explosive energy about 500 times Earth's nuclear arsenal at the height of the Cold War. While the bombardment caused Jupiter little damage—the giant planet is about 11 times larger than Earth—extensive worldwide media coverage gave many people their first look at the realities of cosmic collisions.

returning long enough for astronomers to have calculated their orbits for a long time to come. Long-period comets, however, plunge toward the Sun only once in hundreds or thousands of years. Thus they can come out of nowhere and give only a few months' warning.

If it were determined that an asteroid or comet was on a collision course with Earth, it might be possible to dispatch a space mission to nudge it into a slightly different orbit by means of a nuclear explosive. Exactly how that would be done is not clear, but it is obvious that the first step would be to detect the deadly wanderer. With such relatively small objects it is not easy, but nearly 200 bodies that cross Earth's orbit have already been detected and tracked. Chapman and Morrison mention estimates that virtually all the rest could be found in 30 years by an observational program costing $50 million to start up and a modest $10 million per year to run thereafter.

Chapman and Morrison have therefore accomplished the two main tasks of risk management: they have determined a risk, small though it may be in terms of a human lifetime, and they have described a program for reducing it. As they say, "By choosing whether or not to do something about this threat from the skies, society may establish a standard against which its responses to other hazards are measured." The human population of Earth currently stands at 5.5 billion. If that round number can be taken for purposes of argument, and considering the fact that such a rampage of nature would be capable of killing a substantial fraction of the population, or even all of it, 5.5 billion human beings minus two owe a debt of gratitude to these rational citizens of the planet.

All in all, the human species has triumphed over risk so far. Perhaps we should thank our stars—no, our asteroids and comets—that we have got off as well as we have!

AUTHORS

NATURE ON THE RAMPAGE

H. J. de Blij is the popular Geography Editor of ABC Television's *Good Morning America*, and appears frequently to discuss current events in geographic context. He holds a Ph.D. in geography from Northwestern University, and is Landegger Distinguished Professor of Geography at Georgetown University, on leave from his permanent position at the University of Miami. Professor de Blij is author, co-author, or editor of more than 30 books, and has published more than 100 articles in the professional literature. He is the former editor of the National Geographic Society's scientific journal, *National Geographic Research*.

WEATHER'S FURY

Richard Lipkin is an editor at *Science News* magazine. A graduate of Princeton University, he has been a writer and editor for *The MacNeil/Lehrer Newshour*, United Press International, the *Wilson Quarterly*, and *Insight*. He is the co-author of *Mathematical Impressions* (American Mathematical Society, 1990), the story of Russian artist and mathematician Anatoli Fomenko. Recently he was a fellow at the Knight Center for Specialized Journalism at the University of Maryland, College Park.

FROM ICE TO FIRE

Elizabeth Culotta is a contributing writer and editor at *Science* magazine. A graduate of Yale University, she holds a master's degree in geology from the University of Michigan. She is a former science reporter for the *Milwaukee Journal*, and her work has appeared in *Audubon*, *Earth*, and *Science World* magazines. She has been a science writing fellow at the Marine Biological Laboratory in Woods Hole, Massachusetts, and has received journalism awards from the American Psychological Association, the Education Writers Association, and the National Headliners Club.

THE UNSTABLE EARTH

Richard Monastersky is Earth Sciences Editor of *Science News* magazine, for which he has pursued science stories from the South Pole to Greenland during the past seven years. A Phi Beta Kappa graduate in physics from Wesleyan University, he covers research on earthquakes, volcanoes, environmental issues, and paleontology. His articles and photographs have appeared in *Discover*, *Earth*, *Science World*, encyclopedias, and text books.

THE NATURE OF RISK

Dennis Flanagan is the former editor of *Scientific American*, a position he held for 37 years until retirement in 1984. He is the author of the widely praised *Flanagan's Version: A Spectator's Guide to Science on the Eve of the 21st Century* (Knopf, 1988). A graduate of the University of Michigan, he was on the staff of *Life* from 1941 to 1947. Mr. Flanagan was awarded UNESCO's Kalinga Prize in 1982 for his contributions to the popularization of science. He has been a visiting fellow at several universities, has served as president of the American Society of Magazine Editors, and is a trustee of the New York Hall of Science and a fellow of the American Academy of Arts and Sciences.

SELECTED REFERENCES

WEATHER'S FURY

The Big One: Hurricane Andrew. The Miami Herald. Kansas City, Missouri: Andrews and McMeel, 1992.

Gore, Rick. "Andrew Aftermath." *National Geographic*, Vol. 183, no. 4, April 1993.

The Great Flood of 1993. Natural Disaster Survey Report. Silver Spring, Maryland: National Weather Service, 1994.

Gribbin, John. *Weather Force.* New York: G.P. Putnam's Sons, 1979.

Hall, Roy S. "Inside a Texas Tornado," *Weatherwise*, Vol. 40, no. 2, April 1987.

High and Mighty: The Flood of '93. St. Louis Post-Dispatch. Kansas City, Misouri: Andrews and McMeel, 1993.

Hurricane Andrew: South Florida and Louisiana, August 23-26, 1992. Natural Disaster Survey Report. Silver Spring, Maryland: National Weather Service, 1993.

Inferno. The Orange County Register. Kansas City, Missouri: Andrews and McMeel, 1993.

Jackson, Donald Dale. "When 20 million tons of water flooded Johnstown." *Smithsonian*, Vol. 20, no. 2, May 1989.

Jeffery, David. "Yellowstone: The Great Fires of 1988." *National Geographic*, Vol. 175, no. 2, February 1989.

Ludlum, David M. "The Johnstown Flood," *Weatherwise*, Vol. 42, no. 2, April 1989.

Mairson, Alan. "The Great Flood of '93," *National Geographic*, Vol. 185, no. 1, January 1994.

Rankin, William. "I Rode the Thunder," *The Saturday Evening Post*, October 15, 1960.

Smith, D.K. *Natural Disaster Reduction: How Meteorological and Hydrological Services Can Help.* Geneva, Switzerland: World Meteorological Organization, 1989.

Whipple, A.B.C. *Planet Earth: Storm,* Alexandria, Virginia: Time-Life Books, 1982.

The Widespread November 21-23, 1992 Tornado Outbreak: Houston to Raleigh and Gulf Coast to Ohio Valley, Natural Disaster Survey Report. Silver Spring, Maryland: National Weather Service, 1993.

Williams, Jack. *The Weather Book,* New York: USA Today/Vintage Books, 1992.

FROM ICE TO FIRE

Bonnifield, Paul. *The Dust Bowl: Men, Dirt and Depression,* Albuquerque: University of New Mexico Press, 1979.

Canby, Thomas Y. "El Niño's Ill Wind." *National Geographic,* Vol. 165, no. 2, February 1984.

Climate and History: Studies in past climates and their impact on man. T.M.L. Wigley, M.J. Ingram and G. Farmer, Eds. New York: Cambridge University Press, 1981.

Climate Change 1992. The Supplementary Report to the Intergovernmental Panel on Climate Change Assessment. J.T. Houghton, B.A. Callander, and S.K. Varney, Eds. New York: Cambridge University Press, 1992.

Crowley, Thomas J., and G.R. North. *Paleoclimatology.* Oxford: Oxford University Press, 1991.

Dawson, Alastair G. *Ice Age Earth: Late Quaternary Geology and Climate,* New York: Routledge, Chapman and Hall, Inc., 1992.

The East Bay Hills Fire. Sacramento: State of California, Governor's Office of Emergency Services, February 1992.

El Niño: Historical and Paleoclimatic Aspects of the Southern Oscillation. Henry F. Diaz and Vera Markgraf, Eds. New York: Cambridge University Press, 1992.

Global Climates Since the Last Glacial Maximum. H. E. Wright, Jr. et al., Eds. Minneapolis: University of Minnesota Press, 1993.

Hag, Bilal U. *"Sea Level Rise and Coastal Subsidence: Rates and Threats."* Washington, D.C.: National Science Foundation, December 1993.

Hulme, Michael, and Miock Kelly. "Exploring the links between desertification and climate change." *Environment,* Vol. 35, no. 6, June 1993.

Hurt, R. Douglas. *The Dust Bowl: An Agricultural and Social History.* Chicago: Nelson-Hall Inc., 1981.

Kasting, James F., Owen B. Toon, and James B. Pollack. "How Climate Evolved on the Terestial Planets." *Scientific American,* Vol. 258, no. 2, February 1988.

Parfit, Michael. "The Dust Bowl." *Smithsonian,* Vol. 20, no. 3, June 1989.

The Vinland Sagas: The Norse Discovery of America. Magnua Magnusson and Hermann Palsson, translators. New York: New York University Press, 1966.

THE UNSTABLE EARTH

Decker, Robert W., and Barbara B. Decker. *Mountains of Fire: The Nature of Volcanoes.* Cambridge: Cambridge University Press, 1991.

Fuller, Myron L. *The New Madrid Earthquakes.* Washington, D.C.: U.S. Geological Survey Bulletin no. 94, 1912.

The Great Alaskan Earthquake of 1964. Washington D.C.: National Academy of Sciences, 1970.

The Great Tangshan Earthquake of 1976: An Anatomy of Disaster. New York: Pergamon Press, 1988.

Hansen, Gladys, and Emmet Condon. *Denial of Disaster.* San Francisco: Cameron and Company, 1989.

Hardy, David A., and John Murray. *The Fires Within: Volcanoes on Earth and Other Planets.* Surrey: Dragon's World Ltd., 1991.

Krafft, Maurice. *Volcanoes: Fire From the Earth.* New York: Harry N. Abrams, Inc., 1993.

Luhr, James F., and Tom Simpkin. *Paricutin: The Volcano born in a Mexican Cornfield.* Phoenix: Geoscience Press, Inc., 1993.

Nance, John J. *On Shaky Ground: America's Earthquake Alert.* New York: William Morrow and Company, Inc., 1988.

Nuttli, Otto W. *The 1986 Charleston, South Carolina Earthquake: A 1986 Perspective.* Washington, D.C.: U.S. Geological Survey, 1986.

Penick, James Lal, Jr. *The New Madrid Earthquakes.* Columbia: University of Missouri Press, 1981.

Saul, Eric and Don DeNevi. *The Great San Francisco Earthquake and Fire, 1906.* Millbrae, California: Celestial Arts, 1981.

THE NATURE OF RISK

Fernie, J. Donald. "The Tunguska Event." *American Scientist,* September-October 1993.

Gallant, Roy A. "Journey to Tunguska." *Sky and Telescope,* June 1994.

Hecht, Jeff. "Stony asteroid devastated Siberia." *New Scientist,* January 16, 1993.

PICTURE CREDITS

LEGEND
T   Top
C   Center
B   Bottom
L   Left
R   Right

ABBREVIATIONS
SI   Smithsonian Institution
NASA   National Aeronautics and
    Space Administration
USGS   United States Geological
    Survey

COVER
Warren Faidley/Weatherstock.

FRONT MATTER
P.1 Robert Madden/National Geographic Society; 2-3 Ernst Haas/Magnum Photos; 4-5 David Olsen/Weatherstock; 6-7 Wesley Bocxe/Photo Researchers; 8-9 W. Balzer/Weatherstock; 11 top to bottom: Andy Levin/Photo Researchers; Jim Stratford/Black Star; Richard Olsenius; J. Eyerman/Black Star; James Sugar/Black Star.

NATURE ON THE RAMPAGE
12 Andy Levin/Photo Researchers.

WEATHER'S FURY
20 Jim Stratford/Black Star; 22-23 C.J. Walker/Palm Beach Post; 24-25 Najlah Feanny/Black Star; 26T Robin Moyer/Black Star; 26B A.H. Hasler/NASA Goddard; 27 NASA Johnson Space Center/Roger Ressmeyer/Starlight; 28T Paul Horsted; 28C Robert Hynes/National Geographic Society; 28B SI Archives; 29 Peter Menzel; 30T Ben Van Hook/Black Star; 30C,B Mark Perlstein/Black Star; 31 David Lane/Palm Beach Post; 32 Randy Taylor/Sygma; 33,34 Rob Nelson/Black Star; 34-35 Matt Herron/Black Star; 36T Ben Van Hook/Black Star; 36C,B Tomas Muscionico/Contact Press Images; 37 John Lopinot, Palm Beach Post/Sygma; 38 Ben Van Hook/Black Star; 39 Wingstock/Comstock; 40 Ben Van Hook/Black Star; 41T,B Tomas Muscionico/Contact Press Images; 41C Ben Van Hook/Black Star; 42 Bruce Carter, *Weatherwise* Photo Contest; 43T Robert Hynes/National Geographic Society; 43B Paul Horsted; 44 Edi Ann Otto; 45 Chris Johns/Allstock; 46-47 Peter Willing; 48,49 Chris

Johns/Allstock; 50,51,52,53 Peter Menzel; 54-55 Jim Brandenburg/Minden Pictures; 56C Joe Cempa/Black Star; 56T,56-57 J.B. Diederich/Contact Press Images; 58-59,60T Les Stone/Sygma; 60C Eastcott Momatiuk/Woodfin Camp & Assoc.; 61,62T Les Stone/Sygma; 62C Eastcott Momatiuk/Woodfin Camp & Assoc.; 62B Judy Griesedieck/Black Star; 63 UPI, Bettmann; 64-65 Jim Richardson/West Light; 65T Les Stone/Sygma; 65C Judy Griesedieck/Black Star; 66 Brooks Kraft/Sygma; 66-67 Les Stone/Sygma; 68 Warren Winter/Sygma; 68-69 James Richardson/National Geographic Society; 70T,B Les Stone/Sygma; 70C Judy Griesedieck/Black Star; 71 Cameron Davidson/National Geographic Society; 72 Jim Richardson/West Light; 72-73 Les Stone/Sygma; 74,75 Jim Tuten/Black Star; 76 Anestis Diakopoulos/Stock Boston; 77T Lisa Quinones/Black Star; 77B Dan Mohill/Sygma; 78 Annie Griffiths Belt/National Geographic Society; 78-79 Annie Griffiths Belt.

FROM ICE TO FIRE
80 Richard Olsenius; 82-83 Jay Dickman; 84-85 Chris Johns/Allstock; 86,87 Robert Hynes/National Geographic Society; 88 Sygma; 89L Richard Monastersky; 89R Mark Twickler, Glacier Research Group, University of New Hampshire; 90,91 Steven Raymer/National Geographic Society; 92 Philippe Mazellier; 93 NASA Johnson Space Center; 94 Richard B. Waitt, USGS; 95 Earth Observation Satellite Company; 96 Alex Stewart/Image Bank; 96-97 Bill Garrett; 98 D. Aubert/Sygma; 99 Steve McCurry/Magnum Photos; 100T Chris Johns/Allstock; 100B Library of Congress; 102T Jose Azel/Aurora; 102B Steve McCurry/Magnum Photos; 103 Larry Price/Contact Press Images; 104-105,106, 107 Steve McCurry/Magnum Photos; 108 Michael Yamashita/Woodfin Camp & Assoc.; 108-109 David Burnett/Contact Press Images; 110T Robert Caputo/Aurora; 110B David Burnett/Contact Press Images; 110-111 Les Stone/Sygma; 112 Larry Price/Contact Press Images; 112-113 Robert Caputo/Aurora; 114 Dick Schmidt/Sygma; 115T Rob Nelson/Black Star; 115B J.L. Atlan/Sygma; 116T,C NASA; 116B USGS; 117T Bart Bartholomew/Black Star; 117B Gad Schuster/Contact Press Images; 118-119 David Butow/Black Star; 120 Bill Nation/Sygma; 120-121 David Butow/Black Star; 123T Tina Gerson/Sygma; 123BL Gene

Blevins/Sygma; 123BR Joe and Maria Cempa/Black Star; 124 Martin Rutsdi/Black Star; 124-125 P.F. Bentley/Black Star.

THE UNSTABLE EARTH
126 J. Eyerman/Black Star; 128-129 Ted Soqui/Sygma; 130-131 David Butow/Black Star; 132T Alon Reininger/Contact Press Images; 132C,B Les Stone/Sygma; 133, 134T Ted Soqui/Sygma; 134C,B Lauren Greenfield/Sygma; 135 Les Stone/Sygma; 136 NOAA AVHRR, courtesy Environment Research Institute; 136-137 Robert Caputo/Aurora; 138T Richard Leech/National Geographic Society; 138L Chuck O'Rear/West Light; 138BL, BR Shusei Nagaoka/National Geographic Society; 139 David Parker/Photo Researchers; 140L John Edmond/National Geographic Society; 140R Mehau Kulyk/Photo Researchers; 141 Rob Wood/National Geographic Society; 142 ChinaStock Photo Library; 144 J. Patrick Forden/Sygma; 145 James Sugar/Black Star; 146,148,149TR, C,B Records of the U.S.Senate, Center for Legislative Archives, National Archives/Hugh Talman Photography; 147 Culver Pictures; 149TL UPI, Bettmann; 150T Herman Kokojan/Black Star; 150L,B Barbara Laing/Black Star; 151 Cindy Karp/Black Star; 152, 153 Peter Turnley/Black Star; 154, 155 Marshall Lockman/Black Star; 156 Bishop Museum; 157 Guy Motil/West Light; 158 Kyodo/Uniphoto Press Int'l.; 159 Catherine Devine, Cornell Theory Center; 160-161 FPG; 162-163 Roger Ressmeyer for National Geographic Society; 164 Shusei Nagaoka/National Geographic Society; 165T Wayne McLoughlin/National Geographic Society; 165C Jay Matternes/National Geographic Society; 165B Annie Griffiths Belt/National Geographic Society; 166T Giraudon/Art Resource, NY; 166B, 167 O.L. Mazzatenta/National Geographic Society; 168 John Christiansen/Earth Images; 169 Roger Werth/Woodfin Camp & Assoc.; 170 Ralph Perry/Black Star; 170-171 David Weintraub/Photo Researchers; 172-173 Veroula Dovid/Earth Images; 173 Roger Werth/Woodfin Camp & Assoc.; 174 Robert Madden/National Geographic Society; 175T Bill Thompson/Earth Images; 175C Annie Griffiths Belt/National Geographic Society; 175B Ralph Perry/Black Star; 176T Chip Clark, SI; 176C,B Richard Fiske, SI; 178

Ernest Booth/Earth Images; 178-179 P. Vauthey/Sygma; 180-181 Alberto Garcia/SABA; 181 NASA; 182 SI Archives; 184,185T James Sugar/Black Star; 185C G. Brad Lewis/Tony Stone Worldwide; 185B USGS; 186-187 Ken Sakomoto/Black Star.

THE NATURE OF RISK
188,190-191,190B James Sugar/Black Star; 190T USGS; 192 Steven Raymer/National Geographic Society; 193 Francois Gohier/Photo Researchers; 194T Alon Reininger/Contact Press Images; 194B James Sugar/Black Star; 194-195 Les Stone/Sygma; 196T John Nakata, assisted by D. Hamann, P. Wilshire, D. Prose, USGS/Sight & Sound Productions; 196B David Parker, Science Photo Library/Photo Researchers; 197T Melvin Prueitt, Los Alamos National Laboratory, Data from USGS; 197B James Sugar/Black Star; 198 Steve McCurry/Magnum Photos; 199T Marcus Brooke/FPG; 199B S. Franklin/Magnum Photos; 200,201 Ravi Arya/Black Star; 202 Bill Ross/Woodfin Camp & Assoc.; 203T Mark Wexler/Woodfin Camp & Assoc.; 203C Tom Sobolik/Black Star; 203B Steve Shelton/Black Star; 204-205,205 Peter Menzel; 206 Sisse Brimberg/National Geographic Society; 207T Alon Reininger/Contact Press Images; 207B Steven Raymer/National Geographic Society; 208 Peter Turnley/Black Star; 209T David Strick/Black Star; 209B Rick Browne/Black Star; 210-211 James Baker; 211 Jonathan Blair/Woodfin Camp & Assoc.; 212 Sovfoto; 213T Earth Satellite Corporation; 213BL V.L. Sharpton, Lunar & Planetary Institute; 213BR Kevin Osborn, Research & Design, Ltd.; 214T Jonathan Blair/Woodfin Camp & Assoc.; 214C Dan Haar; 214B Jay Leviton-Atlanta; 215 Jonathan Blair/Woodfin Camp & Assoc.; 216 NASA Goddard from Calar Alto Observatory, Spain; 216-217 Don Davis.

INDEX